TO THE PLACE OF YOUR DREAMS

DREAMS

A Relocation Handbook

TROY HEERWAGEN

Edited by Jennifer Hager
Cover design by Mi Ae Lipe

FIRST EDITION

ISBN-13: 978-0-692-33860-5

ISBN-10: 0692338608

www.ARelocationHandbook.com

Table of Contents

Acknowledgments v

Introduction vii

How to Use This Book xi

RELOCATION IN CONTEXT 1

1   Where You Live Matters 3

CONSIDERING A MOVE 11

2   Think About It 13

3   Develop Your Criteria 21

4   Gather Information 43

5   Evaluate and Decide 57

PREPARING TO RELOCATE 73

6   Plan 75

7   Find a Job 97

8   Find a New Home 113

9   Arrange Your Move 139

10   Say Goodbye 159

MOVING AND ARRIVING 183

11   Pack Up 185

12   Move 197

13   Arrive and Move In 203

14   Settle In and Look Ahead 211

Online Resources 231

Reference Books 245

Works Cited 247

Table of Worksheets

Worksheet: Why You Want To Move 16

Worksheet: Objectives For The Move 17

Worksheet: Criteria 22

Worksheet: Pre-Visit Prep...50

Worksheet: Post-Visit Evaluation 53

Worksheet: Criteria Evaluation 60

Worksheet: Pros and Cons 62

Worksheet: Deconstruct Concerns...64

Worksheet: Opportunity Costs 66

Worksheet: Acknowledge Your Emotions...76

Worksheet: Risk Mitigation Plan 79

Worksheet: Your Plan...86

Worksheet: Your Budget 93

Worksheet: Evaluating a Neighborhood 121

Worksheet: Evaluating a Home 126

Worksheet: Address Change Log 176

Worksheet: To Do Before You Leave 180

Worksheet: Goals And Habits 214

Worksheet: Feelings About New Home...223

Worksheet: Changes After Moving...228

Acknowledgments

This book is dedicated to everyone who has endeavored to make positive change in their lives, whether by refusing to settle for mediocre, starting better habits, or relocating.

I credit the hundreds of people who reached out to us via our blog to spark this book idea. I appreciate the input from the book's mailing list subscribers who responded to surveys, provided feedback, and proofread, particularly Young C. Fan.

My editor, Jennifer Hager, was a great influence towards sharpening the content and invigorating the writing in the book.

I couldn't have done this without my wife, Lesley. In our move from Texas to Seattle, we followed the same process outlined in this book and our lives haven't been the same since.

I also thank my parents—for having me, nurturing me, and supporting me over the years. My moving away was probably one of their least favorite things I ever did, probably even lower on the list than that time I pulled a chair out from under my teacher. But, if I hadn't relocated, I wouldn't be able to thank them in a book.

Introduction

In 2007, my wife and I had just gotten married and decided we would like to live somewhere else. Getting married wasn't enough of a change—we wanted a bigger one: to discover a new area.

Lesley and I were both born in Texas. We grew up a few miles from each other and went to the same high school. Some people chose to go to college out of state, but I didn't have any interest in that. I'd been taught by everyone around me that Texas was possibly *the* best place in the world to live. Why would I ever want to leave? So, I stayed in state for college, attending school in a nearby city.

Whenever I went back home to visit, I'd see friends still working at the same fast food counters they had worked at during high school. I wondered: thirty years from now, will they still be working here? It seemed to me that people with their whole futures ahead of them were treating the future like the past.

And I asked myself: thirty years from now, will *I* still be living nearby, going to these same fast food places? And then the idea came to me that *I could choose to live somewhere else.*

While Texas does have a lot going for it, my wife and I started to get tired of the smothering summer heat. We also felt that the suburban lifestyle we were used to wasn't good for our health or the planet.

We realized it was pretty unlikely that we just happened to be born in the best possible location for us. There might be some other place more in tune with our interests and how we wanted to live our lives. After all, there are millions of other places in the world to live. Deep down, I wanted to stretch myself and discover a place that was completely new to me.

Besides, if we didn't move now as a newly married couple, would we ever have a better time to leave? And if we never left, would we regret the missed opportunity? It seemed like a good idea to get out more on our own and try living somewhere that fit us better.

After reading about numerous places across the country and looking at statistics, we gathered that the Pacific Northwest might better suit us and the life we wanted. We visited and fell in love with the area. The natural beauty and the vibrant urban lifestyle offered by both Seattle and Portland were unlike anything we had seen in Texas. Both looked like the places of our dreams.

While we were drawn to the Pacific Northwest, it was hard to explain our reasons for relocating in terms that everyone could understand. Some people felt Texas's low cost of living plus having family and friends nearby were more than enough reasons to stay where we were.

We knew there would be downsides to relocating and that it would take effort, but we felt that it would be worth it.

Over a period of several months, we worked hard to find jobs in either of the two cities, and eventually Lesley landed a job in Seattle. We lined up movers and arranged a great road trip across the country.

In February 2008, we were on our way.

To stay in touch with family and friends, we published a blog. We posted regularly about our move, the things we did in Seattle, and how our lives were changing. Most of our readers were people we knew. But from time to time, others we'd never met posted comments on our blog.

In the years after our move to Seattle, our online following grew. We received emails from Illinois and Indonesia. People even stopped us on the street in Seattle to tell us how our blog had helped them with their move.

I thought: if our simple blog is this helpful to people moving to Seattle, then a book could be even more helpful to more people moving to more places. The lessons we learned and the process we went through could be valuable to anyone facing a relocation. Millions of people in the United States relocate every year. If this book helps just a fraction of those people to create a better life by relocating, it will be worth it.

In writing this book, I drew from my own experience, the lessons I had blogged about, and conversations with many people who have moved. I assembled research from dozens of websites, moving guidebooks, and migration studies.

The result is a comprehensive resource for anyone contemplating living in a different place. Whether you have just moved or don't have a clue how to start, this book helps you consider all aspects of relocating. It simplifies the moving process, providing you with step-by-step guidance and tools to ensure that your move goes smoothly. It also suggests ways to adjust to your new home.

By relocating, we gained a richer perspective on the world, created some awesome memories, and established the lifestyle we wanted in a place that we love.

I hope that this book helps you achieve whatever it is that you seek in the place of your dreams.

How to Use This Book

This book is divided into four major sections:

- **Relocation in Context**: While writing this book, I discovered that relocation is very common and that where you choose to live has a big impact on your quality of life. Chapter 1 puts your move in a larger context.

- **Considering a Move**: There's a lot to think about when deciding whether or not to relocate and in comparing different locales. I help you identify what's important to you to have in a location and how to find your right place.

- **Preparing to Relocate**: This part of the book walks you through the process of moving, step by step, with extensive information and numerous tips that make moving manageable.

- **Moving and Arriving**: Making the move and settling in is much more than just having a home in a different place. The most challenging (and exciting) part of relocation is adjusting to a new area, putting down roots, and creating a new life. These chapters help you achieve these successful outcomes in your new place.

I share my personal relocation experience in text boxes throughout the book. The book includes a number of exercises to help you organize your thoughts, feelings, questions, preferences, and plans. These worksheets are also available online at www.ARelocationHandbook.com.

I recommend that you read the book once through and bookmark key sections as you go so that you can refer to them later. Each person approaches moving differently, and there may be sections in the book that don't apply to you. You may want to take shortcuts on your journey or proceed through the moving process in a different order than the way things have been presented.

As you go forward with your relocation, you might find it helpful to schedule a time each week to review relevant parts of the book and get pointers for the step you're currently working on.

Use the book in whatever way you find helpful—even to prop your door open on moving day!

RELOCATION IN CONTEXT

1 Where You Live Matters

Migration is a central theme of American history. The arrival of the first Americans from Northeast Asia over 12,000 years ago, the waves of European immigration between the 16th and 19th centuries, the passage of slaves from western Africa, and the drive to conquer the land from coast to coast in the name of "Manifest Destiny" all profoundly influenced the nation and its people.

Today, 42 million people—about *one in seven* Americans—move each year, according to the U.S. Census. And in fact, over 40% of Americans are now living in a different state than where they were born (U.S. Census 2011).

If you're reading this book, perhaps you might become one of them.

REASONS FOR MOVING

People move for different reasons. The largest portion of recent moves from one county to another (35%) was made for job-related reasons, like to take a new job or to look for a new job. Nearly one-third of all moves (31%) were for family-related reasons, like a change in marital status or to move closer to aging parents. Another 31% of movers sought better housing, such as a less expensive home or a nicer neighborhood. Reasons are shown on the following graph (U.S. Census 2013).

Reasons for Moving

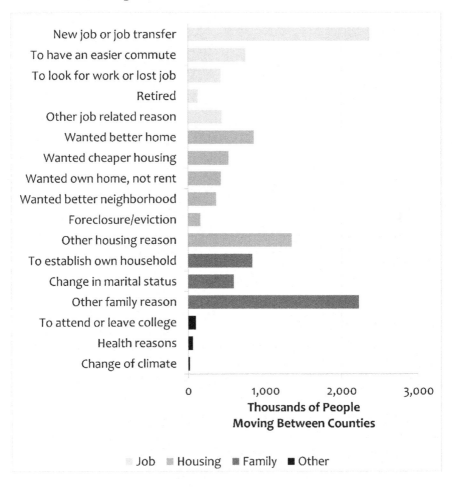

However, the Census only allows respondents to list *one primary reason* for the move. Most moves involve several factors, but those are not recorded. For instance, some people who relocate for a new job only consider jobs in communities that match their values. Other people want to be closer to family but are also attracted by lower housing costs.

LOCATION AFFECTS YOUR OPPORTUNITIES

Advances in technology like teleconferencing, the Internet, and social media have transformed how we access information and made it easy for us to connect with people remotely. However, our physical location is still important.

Almost every person you meet, meal you enjoy, and job you take is likely to be directly related to where you live. Where you live also affects your dating pool and the types of potential partners you'll find.

According to Harvard University psychologist Daniel Gilbert in the book *Stumbling on Happiness,* "Most of us make at least three important decisions in our lives: where to live, what to do, and with whom to do it."

A study by researchers at England's Sheffield University analyzed where people were born and how that related to their health, education, and economic situation. They found that people's birthplace had an impact throughout their entire lives. Researchers concluded that "where you live can limit or assist your life chances from cradle to grave." (Florida 2008)

LOCATION AFFECTS YOUR HAPPINESS

Where you live also influences your happiness. Richard Florida is an urban theorist and the author of several books about urban regeneration. For the book *Who's Your City?,* he conducted the "Place and Happiness Survey" with the Gallup organization to find out how happiness and location of residence are related.

The survey identified five factors of our community that affect our happiness, listed in order of most influence to least. Compare these to the factors that matter most to you:

1. **Aesthetics:** Natural beauty, parks, air quality, climate, and culture. According to Florida, "The higher people rate the beauty of their community, its physical environment, and recreational offerings, the higher their overall level of community satisfaction."

2. **Basic services:** Schools, health care, religious institutions, transportation, and affordable housing.

3. **Security:** Physical security and crime levels as well as financial security, economics, and employment levels.

4. **Openness:** Tolerance and acceptance of diverse groups including families with children, ethnic and racial minorities, the young and the

old, the rich and the poor, LGBT (lesbian, gay, bisexual, and transgender) orientations, and foreign immigrants.

5. **Leadership**: Quality of local political, business, and nonprofit leadership and public engagement.

MOVING AT DIFFERENT STAGES OF LIFE

If the place where you live doesn't currently make you happy or provide the opportunities you want in life, then relocating might be in your best interest.

Your approach to moving is likely related to the stage of life you are in. You may not exactly fit into one of these categories, but in all stages of life, there are reasons to move and reasons not to.

Going Off to College

Going to school further afield can be a great option to consider, either for an undergraduate or graduate program.

It can be tough to leave your support network behind and say goodbye to your parents and old friends. You might ask yourself how comfortable you are being away from your family. Do you feel that you need to come back on weekends, or would you be okay coming back only during holidays?

The sense of adventure and excitement is strong at this time in your life. If you're going to move out of your parents' house anyway, moving further away doesn't require much special effort. You don't even have to make a long-term commitment to a new city, because you can decide where to move again after college is over. Though living on or near campus may keep you insulated from the broader community, attending class gives you structure, and the campus will become a familiar place.

Starting Life Somewhere New

Almost one-third of 20- to 29-year-olds moved in the previous year. This is more than twice the rate of people in all other age groups (U.S. Census 2013).

You likely have the most freedom you've ever had (or will have) in your life, so it can be a good time to try something new. You could have a great time exploring a new city. However, cities popular with young people can often be expensive and tug at your purse springs, making it hard to save any money.

If you're just out of school and need to find a job anyway, why not relocate to a place that appeals to you and look for one there?

> My Experience
>
> *This best describes our situation as we grew up in a place that did not fit what we wanted out of life. Along with thousands of other people who have the freedom to move without too many obligations, we looked for a place that suited us better.*

Pursuing Employment Prospects

You might want to relocate for better opportunities. Perhaps you're being recruited for a job and have to consider a new city in addition to a new job description.

If finding a job is your primary motivation, you might not get to consider other lifestyle preferences like the weather or proximity to family. Your job opportunity may not be in the city of your dreams.

If you're out of work, looking for work *outside* of your current area can be one way to open yourself to more opportunities and possibly land a job more quickly. Different job markets might be a better match for your skills than where you live now.

Since job searches can take a long time, start looking to move as soon as you sense that things might not work out well for you where you are now. Give proper consideration to the cities you're looking at and understand which is more important to you, your career or your lifestyle. If you find an appealing job in an unappealing place, or an unappealing job in an appealing place, is it worth it?

Responding to Family Changes

If changes in family status like marriage, divorce, or having children compel you to move out of your current home, it could be an opportunity to relocate to a more desirable part of the country.

Moving for family reasons can add an additional level of emotion that might make it harder to think through things rationally and be sure that you are making the right decision.

If you have children, consider how relocating will affect the other members of your family. Will another environment be better for them, worse, or just different?

While having children means making a number of compromises in your life, be sure to consider what's best for you as well as what's best for them. Rather than forfeiting your own needs and preferences, seek some middle ground that offers a "win/win" for both you and the kids.

Seeking a Better Fit

Maybe you feel as if you don't belong in your current place anymore. It might be a good time to reassess your life dreams, hopes, and objectives to help determine if relocating is the right answer for you.

If you have a steady job, a home, a weekly routine, and friends or family where you are, it can be difficult to change course. Lacking a strong impetus like graduation or a job hunt, you might not be able to make a leap to a new area. However, having a stable situation may allow you more time to research, gather information, and find the right place!

Entering Retirement

Ready to stop working and want to enjoy your golden years somewhere you've always wanted to live? These days many people officially retire, only to begin new careers or devote themselves to volunteer activities and civic causes. Older adults enjoy "continuing adult education" classes of all types. Many take up creative endeavors that rejuvenate their lives.

Leaving a long-time home and close friends can be emotionally difficult. Moving at an older age—and generating new relationships in a new place—can be challenging. However, settling in a new place can open possibilities in every area of life.

There are many retirement communities where you can meet others looking for the same things. And not having to work means that you'll really have time to enjoy where you're living.

Moving without a Choice

You may need to relocate against your will. This can happen with the death of a close family member, a natural disaster, a foreclosure, or unfair persecution.

At any stage of life, making good decisions can be hard work. When you're stressed or emotionally depleted, decision-making is much harder. You might have to dig deep within yourself to find enough mental energy to identify a place where you would like to live.

Ask yourself, how permanent is the move? Would you want to move back to your home after some time away?

If you're depressed, moving can help get you out of a rut, but don't hesitate to seek help from others. Even if some things are out of your control, look for areas in which you can actively make decisions.

While this can be hard to recognize at the time, *great challenges can also be great opportunities*. Even if moving is unwanted, it could bring a better outcome than staying put. Moving can help during a grieving process and can be an opportunity to put painful parts of the past behind you.

Take heart that things will get better. Life has a way of balancing out over time.

• • •

Whatever your reasons, relocating takes you down a different path than the one you're on. Changing where you live has the potential to transform your life in amazingly positive ways.

CONSIDERING
A MOVE

2 Think About It

The urge to make a change may manifest itself in different ways. It could be restlessness in your free time, disgust on your drive home, embarrassment when reading the news, or a growing dissatisfaction with the path your life is on.

Regardless of what drives your interest in moving, let's explore this further.

CONSIDERING RELOCATION

Perhaps Mark Twain said it best: "Twenty years from now you will be more disappointed by the things that you didn't do than by the ones you did do. So throw off the bowlines. Sail away from the safe harbor. Catch the trade winds in your sails. Explore. Dream. Discover."

It's a Big Decision

However, deciding whether to pack up and move away from your home—whether it's been your home for six months or 60 years—is a life-changing decision and easier said than done. You're reaching a fork in the road and

13

relocating can be like choosing the less-traveled path in an unfamiliar direction with an unclear destination.

Once you move, every new person you meet, every new restaurant you try, and every sunset you watch will happen for you because you're in this new place. Conversely, in the place you've left behind, there will be people you'll never get to meet, dogs you won't get to pet, and local news broadcasts you won't get to watch.

However, this is similar to other trade-offs we make in life. Every decision presents the possibility of a better future, but with a cost of a lost opportunity. Ordering stir-fry for lunch means you won't get to try the won tons. Fortunately, unlike won tons, moving is life-changing.

MY EXPERIENCE

One of my favorite sculptures is Eagle by Alexander Calder. This sculpture used to be in the middle of downtown Fort Worth when I was growing up. When I moved to Seattle, I discovered that it was the centerpiece of Seattle's Olympic Sculpture Park.

As with other sculptures, you can't see it all by staying in the same spot. It looks different when you look at it from different angles. It looks different in different settings. It looks a lot different near Seattle's Elliott Bay than it did near an office tower in Fort Worth.

Your life is a sculpture and you're the artist: you won't see it all if you stay in the same spot.

Emotions and Feelings

The idea that a "perfect" place exists is a myth; you may be able to lead a happy, fulfilling life in a number of different places.

The perfect place for your career, for your family, and for your recreation might be three different places. We humans are complicated with varying and sometimes conflicting desires in life.

As German author Christian Morgenstern said, "Home is not where you live but where they understand you."

Is a new home going to be better enough to justify relocating? There will be trade-offs, and it's important to be aware that there may be drawbacks. Even the place we identify as best for us could be worse in some ways than where we live now.

When you move, people won't know who you are, and your identity may change as you open to a new environment and new people. How important is your city to your identity? Today are you proud to be in a small town? How will you feel as a resident of your new city? How else will moving change your identity—will you lose a reputation you've earned? Or will you take the opportunity to be more authentic to yourself?

If you have moved previously in your life, explore your history. How did the relocation affect your circumstances? How did you feel about it? Anxious? Conflicted? Excited?

YOUR PERSONAL VALUES

Many decisions you make in life are consciously or subconsciously based on your underlying values. With such a significant decision as relocating, you need to be aware of what those values are.

American culture values fun and excitement. Some cultures value stability and family. Are you looking for wealth and status? Do you want close ties and support networks? Do you seek growth and development that leads to accomplishment—or a life of joy and love?

Whatever values define your personal worldview should be taken into account as you consider whether to move. In some cases you could feel coerced into relocating by friends, family, or society—but look deeper into yourself to be sure that this decision truly aligns with where your heart lies.

YOUR OBJECTIVES FOR THE MOVE

You're probably looking to find the "best" place to move to, but what does that really mean?

Think about why you are moving. Try to understand clearly why you want to relocate. Is it just to escape a problem? Or do you know what you want and just need to be in the right place to find it?

Use the following Worksheet to help articulate your thoughts and feelings about moving.

WORKSHEET: WHY YOU WANT TO MOVE

Search your feelings and desires to come up with all the reasons why you think you want to move:

_____

_____

_____

_____

_____

_____

_____

_____

_____

Name all of your concerns and fears about moving:

_____

_____

_____

_____

_____

_____

_____

_____

To help you identify what type of place you're looking for, try to define your objectives for the move. Your objectives are tied to your values. For example, your objective in relocating might be to challenge and stretch yourself because you value a stimulating life. Or your objective could be to advance your career because you value accomplishment.

To help you understand your objectives, review your reasons for moving and express those desires in terms of objectives. What do you expect to find by relocating?

WORKSHEET: OBJECTIVES FOR THE MOVE

Objective	Value that influences this
e.g., Find a better paying job	Financial security
_____	_____
_____	_____
_____	_____
_____	_____
_____	_____
_____	_____
_____	_____

BENEFITS OF MOVING

Moving is a lot of work, there's no denying that. Settling in somewhere new can also be a challenge, straining relationships and budgets. However, the very process of moving and adjusting to a new location has great potential benefits.

- **Gaining skills and confidence:** There are countless details to coordinate as part of a move. Handling these can help you build skills in planning and organizing. You will also gain experience in working with service providers like movers, utilities, and leasing agents. Furthermore, you develop self-confidence by conducting the move yourself.

- **Wisdom and perspective:** Moving will widen your sense of possibility and spur your own mental, physical, and emotional change and growth. By relocating, you will see new environments, meet new people, learn new things, and become aware of a wider world. This experience can make you question your assumptions and open yourself to different ideas and values.

- **Adapt outside of your comfort zone**: Acclimating yourself to a new environment will force you to be flexible to accommodate all the changes.

- **Variety and new experiences**: If variety is the spice of life, then relocation can be a spicy dish! Whether you like your food mild or hot, living somewhere new will expose you to new experiences.

- **Expand your social circle**: Being in a new place brings you in touch with new acquaintances and friends.

- **Prevent regret**: Maybe you don't want to wonder "what if" and would rather extend into whatever unknowns lie ahead in a new place.

In short, facing challenges in life usually makes one stronger. There are many of these associated with moving: in the preparation, the logistics, the stress of relocating, and then adjusting to a new place. There is also a lot to gain.

REASONS TO STAY PUT

While relocating can be a good idea for many reasons, it's not always the best thing to do. If you feel hesitant to move, there might be valid reasons holding you back.

- **Timing**: Even if you want to live in a different place, it's possible that now isn't the best time to do so. Maybe you need to finish school first, pay off your loans, or wait until a better time to leave your job.

- **Not within your means**: Be sure that you're financially prepared for a move. To help you determine if you can afford to relocate, see Worksheet: Your Budget in Chapter 6.

- **Attachment to people**: Being near family and friends, seeing them regularly, and having close, supportive relationships can make all the difference to your happiness. If your family and friends are all nearby today, you won't be able to bring them all with you. Chapter 3 suggests some aspects of being close to family that you can mull over.

- **Attachment to a place**: Many people are tied to the place where they live—whether by desire to stay or fear of change. Review the Worksheet: Why You Want to Move to explore your feelings more carefully.

- **Not suited to your personality**: Moving is considered the third most stressful event in a person's life, behind divorce and death of a loved one. Many stressors occur in the moving process, including change, loss of control, immersion in the unfamiliar, financial impacts, and disruption of routine.

Consider how you deal with stress. Are you prone to find fault and complain? Or can you find excitement and learn to appreciate your new place?

Transplanting yourself will likely shake your composure. However, the moving steps laid out in this book and tips for adjusting to a new home could help you feel more comfortable about the prospect.

- **Not worth it:** While moving could sound like a great opportunity, it's not a cure-all. By moving, you won't suddenly become a different person or solve problems from your past. Money can't buy happiness and neither can relocation. As they say, "The grass is always greener on the other side." There is information in Chapter 3 to help you develop your criteria for a destination, guidance in Chapter 4 for gathering information, and then tools to evaluate what would fit you best in Chapter 5.

- **Happy where you are:** Perhaps after reevaluating your reasons to leave, you might realize you're already in a good place. Why change what you're content with?

There is also the risk that relocating can make your life messy. Adjusting to a new place may require compromises, and things don't always "fall into place" the way we imagined them.

You may settle in a new place only to feel like an outsider for quite a while. And years later, if you return to your hometown, you could have a tough time adjusting back.

What if you move somewhere and meet someone you love, but then family needs pull you back home?

Alfred Lord Tennyson wrote in 1850: " 'Tis better to have loved and lost than never to have loved at all." Perhaps the same thing applies to moving: if you find a place that you love living in, even briefly, that's better than never to have known about it.

• • •

By recognizing your own values and what you hope to gain by moving, you will be able to approach this topic with a clearer head.

3 Develop Your Criteria

There are many websites and rankings that will tell you the best places to live in the country, but if you look a little deeper you'll find that those "bests" don't necessarily apply to you. Each person has unique desires, and identifying your own criteria will help you arrive at the right place.

Yogi Berra said, "If you don't know where you are going, you'll end up someplace else."

Does the city of your dreams have mountains and water, like mine did? Or do you dream of a lower cost of living, high-tech job opportunities, or living near more people like yourself?

Look a few years ahead too. How do your criteria change if you're planning to get married, have children, or retire?

It may take some introspection to acknowledge what is really important to you. Use the following Worksheet: Criteria to help organize your thoughts.

WORKSHEET: CRITERIA

Use this worksheet to rank your main criteria for a new place. Group your criteria into sections based on what's important to you.

e.g., Location: Near a major airport

e.g., Climate: Warm winters

Must Haves—critical needs for your new home

1. _____

2. _____

3. _____

4. _____

5. _____

6. _____

Should Have—what you would really like to have in your new home

7. _____

8. _____

9. _____

10. _____

11. _____

12. _____

Nice to Have—what you could have if possible

13. _____

14. _____

15. _____

16. _____

17. _____

18. _____

Must Not Have—things that are completely undesirable to have in your new home

19. _____

20. _____

21. _____

22. _____

23. _____

24. _____

BASIC NEEDS

If you're looking for an area where you can earn an income and live affordably and safely, consider these basics.

Economy and Employment

If you don't have a job or are looking for a better job, finding a good economy may be paramount. Nearly one-fourth of the people who are moving between counties do so because of a company transfer, to start a new job, or to seek a new job (U.S. Census 2013).

If you will be looking for work in your new home, consider what field you want to work in. While a variety of opportunities exist in most parts of the country, certain areas are better for people who want to excel in a particular field. Very successful people are often clustered together, from innovators in Silicon Valley to filmmakers in Hollywood. Marketable skills, experience, and persistence can take you far, but it would be wise to be employable in any destinations you consider.

Key Information

- **Unemployment rate and job growth**: The unemployment rate is a simple metric that reflects economic vitality. Looking at the number of people employed and how that number has changed can suggest how strong the local economy is, and where it's headed.

  The Bureau of Labor Statistics releases monthly unemployment information by state and city, which is called "civilian labor force and unemployment by state and metropolitan area." www.bls.gov/web/metro/laummtrk.htm shows unemployment percent by city.

- **Top industries and top employers:** If the industry you want to work in is strong in a locale, you're more likely to be able to find a job and advance. For example, 75% of entertainers and performers work in Los Angeles, and 78% of political scientists work in Washington, D.C. (Florida 2008). Also look into the top employers in each city—are they successful and growing, or have they had layoffs? Would you want to work for any of these employers? You can often find the top employers in an area's economy from Wikipedia or other online sources.

- **Contacts:** How many professional contacts do you know in a city? The most common way for people to find a job is by talking to people they know, so having connections in an area greatly increases your chances of securing employment. If you don't know people there, maybe someone you know does and can help you make local connections.

Cost of Living

How far you can stretch your dollars is greatly affected by how many thousands of those dollars will go towards your living expenses.

You might see all cities as basically equivalent—they all have places to live, grocery stores, and restaurants—so why would you pay more to live in one over another?

Places that cost more to live in provide a higher quality of life that's worth the added cost to some people. More expensive cities often have more economic opportunity, better weather, or more cultural vibrancy. "You get what you pay for" can ring true if you've found one of those places that fits you.

It's important to know what you can afford. The rule of thumb is that your housing costs shouldn't exceed 30% of your income, though that rule can be hard to follow in cities like San Francisco and New York. If you're willing to cut costs in other areas of your life, you might be able to afford an expensive area, but be sure you know what you're getting into. Find out whether new taxes or local laws will affect your estate planning or retirement income. Also be sure to factor in all costs such as additional commute time, child care, or increased heating and cooling costs.

My Experience

After moving to Seattle, a common thing we were asked by friends and family in Texas was: "How much does gas cost?" While gas prices were about 40 cents higher in Seattle, our transportation costs were much lower since we sold one car and drove much less often.

You will likely need to create a budget of your anticipated personal expenditures and research the cost of living you can afford.

Key Information

- **Cost of living**: Each city has its own price index. Look at things like the costs of housing (renting or buying), groceries and eating out, utilities, health care, and transportation.

  There are websites that provide a cost of living calculator in different cities or compare the costs of living between different cities. For example: www.bankrate.com/calculators/savings/moving-cost-of-living-calculator.aspx and www.numbeo.com.

- **Income for your position**: People doing the same job earn different amounts in different areas. Areas with a higher cost of living generally pay higher wages, though usually not enough to compensate completely for the increased cost of living. The wages paid can also vary based on local competition for employment or for employees.

  There are sites online like www.salary.com and www.indeed.com that provide information on what your job title would fetch in different areas.

- **Taxes**: How taxes are collected varies widely. Some areas have sales tax but no income tax; others have income tax but no sales tax. While tax rates vary by state, you could think about which tax structure works best for you. For example, if you spend a lot of money but want to have a modest home, then perhaps a state with high property tax but low sales tax would suit your budget well. This website has information on different tax rates by state and down to the county level: www.tax-rates.org

- **Regulations and legal protections**: If you are a small business owner, your business can be affected by local or state government regulations that restrict how you do business or protections that affect your legal liability. Research any laws related to your line of work on the state or local government websites.

Crime and Safety

Statistically, you probably won't be a victim of crime, but where you live affects the odds. Crime rates can vary between personal crimes like assault and robbery or property crimes like home burglary and car theft. Living in a rough area can challenge your emotions and sense of security on a daily basis, especially if you have children.

However, there are safe areas in every city and dangerous areas in most cities and many towns, so crime statistics aren't always valuable in assessing an area's safety. You might also want to factor in other aspects of safety, such as weather and natural disasters like hurricanes, floods, ice storms, earthquakes, and volcanic eruption.

Key Information

- **Crime data:** There are a few sources of crime statistics; however looking at a single metric of crime illustrates the limitations of data. Many cities have areas that range from very safe to very unsafe, so a "total" safety number won't give a perspective of that range. Here are some resources:

    o **FBI Uniform Crime Reporting:** Crimes are tracked by local police departments and reported to the FBI. Many websites use this information to compare crime statistics between cities.

    o **National Crime Victimization Survey:** NCVS determines crime rates and types of crimes committed based on interviews with citizens. The NCVS might include crimes not reported to police; however, it excludes some types of crime like homicides as well as arson and other commercial crimes.

    o **Crime maps:** There are websites that map specific locations of crimes in different cities, for example www.spotcrime.com and www.trulia.com/crime. Areas where more people live, work, and play such as central business districts usually have more crime. This type of source could be helpful if you're looking to find areas in cities with *low* crime. You could also look at areas where you'd be likely to spend time including employment centers or neighborhoods you might want to live in.

- o **News:** Local news is one way to gather information on crime, but consider the sensationalistic approach to reporting that many media sources take. Most metropolitan areas have dangerous areas that appear frequently in the news.

- o **Local perspective:** Ask people in the area where the safer and more dangerous parts of town are.

- **Weather risk:** Since natural disasters often don't recur in a specific area, it can be hard to evaluate the risk of hurricanes, tornadoes, and earthquakes. The New York Times created an evaluation of natural disaster risk:

  www.nytimes.com/interactive/2011/05/01/weekinreview/01safe.html

SERVICES

A robust array of local services can improve the quality of your life, providing quality healthcare, adequate transportation infrastructure, and education opportunities.

Health

If you have disabilities, some cities are more likely than others to have treatment available and be built around your needs. Or, you may participate in a health routine that has specific needs.

In addition to looking at health services offered in an area, you might contemplate your ability to live a healthy lifestyle. If you're exposed to a culture where people make healthy lifestyle decisions, you're more likely to do so as well. Your idea of a healthy city could include healthy eating options at grocery stores and restaurants and outdoor recreational activities. You may look for comfortable outdoor weather, if you'll want to walk as a primary mode of transportation. The quality of the air you breathe and water you drink influences your health as well.

Key Information

- **Air quality:** Knowing the amount of airborne pollutants can help you make an informed decision. www.stateoftheair.org and www.airnow.gov are good resources.

- **Drinking water quality report:** Water utilities are required to create a report on water quality. Many municipalities maintain online reports about what chemicals and pollutants exist in the local water supply.

- **Life expectancy:** Life expectancy varies in different parts of the country, based on lifestyle choice, natural environment, and healthcare options. This visualization can help you see how that number varies: vizhub.healthdata.org/us-health-map/

- **Emergency services:** Being somewhere quickly accessible by emergency services like police, fire, and rescue, as well as having a hospital nearby with a Level 1 Trauma center, can improve your chances of surviving a medical emergency.

- **Number of doctors:** A government council that reported to the U.S. Department of Health and Human Services recommends that a given region have 60 to 80 primary care doctors and 85 to 105 specialists per 100,000 residents (Council on Graduate Medical Education 1996). The Dartmouth Atlas of Healthcare provides a map that shows the number of doctors by region:
  www.dartmouthatlas.org/data/map.aspx?ind=143

Transportation

Traffic is one thing that people rank high on their list of daily inconveniences, and a long commute is linked to obesity and heart disease. While any big city will have heavy traffic, your routines and where you live within that city will determine whether traffic is a problem for you.

Are you tempted to rely on public transportation? Maybe you want to avoid car traffic altogether and live in a city with a robust rail network or good bus systems. Or, do you desire open country roads and freedom from city traffic in a rural area?

Key Information

- **Infrastructure:** Transportation infrastructure can vary appreciably in age, reliability, and comfort from city to city. Does the area have adequate sidewalks and bike lanes? If you expect to be driving, are the roadways built to be traveled at a safe speed and is signage clear?

- **Modal share:** Knowing how people commute, whether by driving, biking, walking, taking transit, or other methods, can help you understand what options will be most available to you in a city. Refer to Wikipedia at:

en.wikipedia.org/wiki/Transportation_in_the_United_States and
en.wikipedia.org/wiki/Modal_share for international information.

> MY EXPERIENCE
>
> *One of the most important things to us was to be able
> to get around by walking and public transportation. To
> identify these places, we looked for cities where the
> modal share showed a low percentage of people who
> commute by driving alone.*

- **Public transportation:** What types of transit infrastructure exist in an area? Are there buses, commuter rail, light rail, or streetcars? Is service frequent and reliable? Check the area's transit maps and note that some cities are served by multiple transit agencies.

- **Alternative transportation services:** Having various ways to get around can make it easier to do without a car. Does your city have bike-share or car-share options?

- **Walk Score:** This website got its start by identifying how easily you can run errands by foot based on the address you provide. Additionally, Walk Score evaluates walkability by neighborhood and city and includes scores for the convenience of bicycling and the frequency of transit service in an area. See www.walkscore.com.

- **Traffic websites:** Consult a traffic website like Google Maps at maps.google.com, a local website provided by a state department of transportation, or a news website during rush hour to find out how many of the roadways are congested.

Education

Excellent public and private schools aren't available just anywhere. School quality could be a primary factor for parents of school-age children and it also affects home resale value.

If you're looking to go to a university, finding the right university might be more important than the city itself. Or maybe you're looking for a graduate program, continuing education options, seminars, or local colleges that offer weekend courses.

Key Information

- **Test results:** Standardized testing is a common way to evaluate students and the quality of education. Test scores can be misleading and don't provide a complete picture of the quality of education. It's worth asking administrators what they focus on and how they determine whether they're providing a quality education.

  States often issue annual scorecards on school districts and individual schools. These school report cards include numbers of teachers and students, standardized test results, teacher education levels, attendance, and breakdown of expenditures. Additionally, the Nation's Report Card scores students in various subjects. The performance scores of students across states, in major cities, as well as the change in scores over time, are all available through the Nation's Report Card. www.nationsreportcard.gov

- **Online reviews:** Some websites provide information on schools based on parent reviews. For example, GreatSchools at www.greatschools.org provides a rating based on a school's test scores and allows parents to evaluate their children's schools based on the principal's leadership ability, the skills of the teachers, strength of the community, and other factors.

- **Practical elements:** Review practical aspects, like the distance between the school and your potential home or place of business, any specific needs your child may have that require special attention, and the structure of the school year (e.g., year-round or traditional). For private schools, check tuition costs.

- **Good fit for your children:** People learn differently, and some types of schooling environments won't work as well for your children as others. Understanding your children and their specific needs can help you look for a learning environment that best helps grow their strengths and overcome their weaknesses.

- **Educational philosophy:** Are you looking for a traditional schooling program or a more innovative approach to learning? Waldorf or Montessori schools won't be available in every area. The same is true of private schools provided by a specific religious denomination. What will the school do if your child is either ahead or behind the pace set by the teacher? How much homework is there?

- **District and school websites:** Websites provide basic details like contact information and schedules but also might give you insight into whether school assignment is based on your address or by lottery, how many schools exist in the district, and how diverse the student body is. For charter schools, you could look into the history and focus of the school, and whether the school's location is permanent.

- **Teachers:** What is the student/teacher ratio? What are the teachers' qualifications? What is the rate of faculty turnover?

- **Resources and relationships:** Look into the availability of counselors, nurses, and librarians. Also, what technology resources are used in the classroom and available to students outside of the classroom? How does the school involve parents?

- **Other parents:** Look into the Parent Teacher Organization (PTO) or Parent-Teacher Association (PTA) so that you can contact parents and ask them directly about the school.

- **Discipline, bullying, and safety:** Find out the school rules and methods of discipline. Are the rules fair and the consequences reasonable? How does the school protect children from bullying? What policies are in place for safety and how are parents notified in case of emergency?

- **Visit schools:** Before choosing a school, visit at least a couple schools to observe how students and teachers behave and what the environment is like.

- **University criteria:** Choosing a university is a bit more complex but can include many similar criteria already covered. If you're looking to earn a degree, you might want to consider the size of the school, the courses of study and degrees available, the quantity and quality of the faculty, and the school's reputation. Numerous college rankings exist and scores of data are available to provide more insight on comparing colleges.

- **Professional development options:** This could include graduate programs, continuing education options, seminars, and local colleges that offer weekend courses. Check the websites of the closest colleges for available courses.

LIFESTYLE

These criteria can help you find the right amenities to suit the lifestyle you'd like to be able to enjoy in your new area.

City Size and Density

Because of the stark differences between cities and rural areas, many people know right away what size city they want to live in. Some people want the bustle of a big city and others want to get away from it. A city's size usually relates to other criteria. For example, big cities usually cost more and have more traffic, public transportation, employment options, and pollution than smaller cities. Cities draw people in to take advantage of the benefits of being close to many things; smaller towns offer more open space and clean air.

Key Information

- **City or metro area population:** Do you want something bigger or smaller than where you live now? A megalopolis or a small town? Be aware that population statistics can be misleading. For example, sprawling Houston has more than two and a half times as many people within the city proper as San Francisco does, but Houstonians are spread over thirteen and a half times the space.

  Knowing a city's population as well as the metro area population is helpful in separating cities into sizes of large, medium, and small. This designation can give you a sense of what big-city amenities to expect. Do you want major league sports teams and a stunning skyline? Or just the basics of life that any town can provide?

- **Density:** The number of people per square mile can be a better guide than size for how a city will feel. Density isn't a perfect metric as it can be skewed by large bodies of water within the city limits that artificially lower the density or by tight city boundaries that exclude a lot of lower density areas in the periphery. It's still a useful metric for you to gauge whether you're more likely to find high rises or sprawling homesteads. Population metrics from the U.S. Census are relatively easy to find online.

Climate

The weather is something we can all complain about, regardless of where we live. Some of us prefer often-sunny Southern California or the dry heat of Arizona. With some of the hottest years on record occurring in the last decade, global climate change will likely continue to influence local weather conditions.

If you're outside a lot, or want to be, a region's climate may be critical. Even if you're not an outdoors person, be aware of how the climate could affect you. For example, dry air can cause flaky skin and inflamed sinuses; wind and rain can aggravate allergies; heat can cause headaches; and cold can cause arthritic aches. Being under cloudy skies all the time can literally be depressing as anywhere from 1.4 to 9.7% of Americans are affected by Seasonal Affective Disorder, which causes depression during winter months due to lower exposure to sunlight (Friedman 2007).

> MY EXPERIENCE
>
> *While cloudy winter months weren't our preference, the moderate weather in the Pacific Northwest was one major advantage Seattle had over locales with more extreme seasonal variations. Based on our time in Texas, hot summers were out of the question, and the snowy winters of the Northeast pushed us away from cities in that area.*

Key Information

There are many weather almanacs online with historical average and record information that you can use to get a better feel for the weather in an area, such as www.cityrating.com/weather-history/. Here are some of the measurables:

- **Rainfall:** Do you like the greenery that the rain provides or prefer to live somewhere dry? Do you have any allergies to mold?

- **Snowfall:** Do you find snow like in the Upper Midwest or New England to be beautiful and fun or an annoying obstacle? In some cities, citizens are required by law to keep their sidewalk shoveled clear.

- **Sunny days:** Are you a sun god and prefer the desert Southwest or Inland Northwest climate, or do you find clouds of the Pacific Northwest comforting? Do you have skin that is at high risk for skin cancer?

- **Average July high:** Are 90 degree summer days of the Deep South and Southwest warm and pleasant or hot and stifling? Homes in some parts of the country don't have or need home air conditioning—does that appeal to you?

- **Average January low:** Is feeling cold miserable or just a sign of being dressed inappropriately?

- **Variety:** To some, year-round warm sunny weather is ideal, so Hawaii or Southern California might appeal. Others like the change of seasons. You might want to look for a variance between winter weather averages and summer weather.

- **Allergens:** If you have to endure seasonal allergies, look for a place with a paucity of pollen. The Asthma and Allergy Foundation of America operates www.allergycapitals.com, which identifies places that are the most and least challenging to live in for allergy sufferers.

- **Visit:** Check out your city in bad weather and good weather if you can. A sunny and warm July in Seattle is a far cry from a cloudy and dark January. Similarly, a sunny and warm December in Dallas gives a different impression than a triple-digit Texas summer.

Recreational Opportunities and Services

Every area has its own take on recreation, whether the local recreation is river rafting, skiing, watching sporting events, or sitting on the porch drinking iced tea. For people whose hobbies are an important part of their lives, this could be an important thing to consider.

Look for references online to find the best areas for hiking, descriptions of hunting conditions in different areas, or cities with the best fine arts available. Just searching an online map or directory can show you if there are enough nightclubs, bait and tackle stores, or shopping malls in a particular city.

Key Information

- **Arts and culture:** Look at listings of the top local arts venues or check out online cultural listings to get a feel for what a city has to offer. Consider what type of cultural experiences you're looking for. Are you looking for local galleries and museums? Many cities have art or history museums, but museums in San Francisco and Washington, D.C. are larger and more highly acclaimed than those in most small towns. What about architecture? Chicago's high on that list. Are you looking for a good public library system, unique bookstores, and literary events you can find in Boston and Portland? How about the top-notch symphony orchestras of Chicago, New York, or Philadelphia? What about excellent artistic performance that New York and Los Angeles are known for?

- **In-town entertainment:** Do you want touring musical acts, live shows, good restaurants and bars, ballroom dancing, or other entertainment? Again, larger cities will have more options than smaller ones, but entertainment options vary by area.

- **Outdoor activities:** The best places for camping, hunting, boating, fishing, hiking, or biking will vary. You won't find beaches and surfing in the Midwest nor skiing in the Deep South.

- **Participating in or watching sports:** You can participate in sports anywhere, but the options will differ based on where you are. Each part of the country has a different set of sports that are its most popular. If you like to watch sports, select cities that host major league teams.

- **Shopping:** Some areas have bigger malls and more shopping opportunities whether because of the economy, demographics, or the culture. Do you want high-end boutiques, local artisan shops, major malls, or discount deals?

- **Animals:** Dog parks are increasingly popular. Alternatively, you can find a home with a big yard. Do you want to own acres of property for horses or other animals?

- **Volunteer work:** If volunteering is an important part of your lifestyle, look for volunteering options. The number of residents who volunteer can range from less than 20% to over 40%. Volunteering in America (www.volunteeringinamerica.gov/rankings.cfm) provides rankings of volunteerism by state. Some areas low in volunteering rates are higher in charitable giving. www.philanthropy.com/article/Interactive-How-America-Gives/133709 shows giving rates.

Aesthetics

An attractive locale is one to be proud of, whether it is due to natural beauty, a litter-free downtown, or carefully maintained lawns and gardens.

Key Information

Beauty is in the eye of the beholder and isn't easily quantifiable. To evaluate the beauty of an area, you might visit or rely on online photos and aerial and street views made available through online mapping tools.

- **Natural scenery:** Locate national parks, state parks, county and municipal parks in an area. Research wildlife preserves and protected habitats.

- **Human-made scenery:** Cities can provide beautiful scenery through their public art and architecture. Consider whether your eyes are drawn to varied and magnificent skylines, painted murals, historical brick buildings, or flowering public gardens.

- **Cleanliness:** Consider the health risks of smog in the air, trash on the ground, or oil in the water. A homeless population that sleeps in public parks or sidewalks could detract from the clean, orderly life you want.

Location

The location of your dot on the map, and its proximity to other dots on the map could be important. How close is a major airport? Is the college you want to attend close enough to drive home for weekends or holidays? Do you want to be politically active in a swing state in the presidential elections?

Key Information

A map is going to be a great tool for you to narrow down your options. You might want a big United States map that you can put pins in, or an online map, to identify key locations. Here are some things to consider:

- **Distance from family and friends:** Put dots on the map where you have family members and friends. How far away do you want to be from family and friends? How often you would you like to visit? How much would a round-trip visit cost?

- **Major airport:** Knowing where the closest major airports are and what nonstop flights are available can help you determine how connected you are to the rest of the world.

- **Proximity to services:** If you're planning to live somewhere rural, how close do you want to be to the services of a large town or city?

PEOPLE

Finding a place with the type of people and culture you want to live near can be very important.

Relationships

Living near family can affect one's life satisfaction. A 2007 study by University of London economist Nattavudh Powdthavee found that the value of seeing family and friends regularly is worth $168,000 in additional annual income (Powdthavee 2007).

Think about the benefits of having people you can rely on to babysit your children, help work on your car, and cook dinner on occasion. Family is a foundation that can provide companionship and emotional support.

On the other hand, family obligations can make you feel tied down if you're seeking freedom. In some cases, close relations can be bad influences.

Regardless of your reasons for moving elsewhere, your transition to a new place can be eased by having an aunt, cousin, or old roommate in the area.

When other people are involved, the situation can be tricky, so make sure everyone has appropriate expectations before moving. For example, conflict could ensue if you are hoping to see your grandchildren daily but your children have other ideas. Sharing your feelings early on is one way to give people time to warm up to an idea and build alignment.

Also, develop a long-term plan. Suppose you move in order to help an elderly parent. When they require placement in a nursing home or if their health improves, what will you do next? If you move to join a romantic relationship that later fizzles out, what will you do?

> ## My Experience
>
> *While our journey to Seattle took us away from many close family members and friends and reduced how frequently we see those people, the distance has transformed our relationships in positive ways. One way is that instead of routinely eating together, we now set aside larger chunks of time for family and friends to visit or for us all to go on vacation together.*

Key Information

Here are some factors to consider when choosing whether to move closer to or farther from family or friends:

- **Orientation to independence and connection:** How important are people in your life? Will you miss people or have no problem making close relationships with others?

- **Your dreams:** Dreams and expectations for your future can be helpful to factor in. Do you want to raise a family close to relatives? Do you want to be more independent?

- **Ability to stay in contact**: If you move, will you make regular visits to people you are leaving behind? Could you call or participate in online video chats with them?

- **Support, influence, and resources**: How much do you rely on and support each other? Do family members support you either through advice, influence, gifts, or financial support? Do you provide vital companionship or guidance to others? If family or friends try to influence your decision, is it for their interest or yours?

- **Personal ads**: If you're looking for a primary relationship in a new place, checking out profiles on online dating sites might help you get a feel for the types of people in a new area.

Local Culture

The culture of an area can be complicated to understand. You can glimpse aspects of culture by finding out how an area voted in the last election or reviewing census data that identifies religious attitudes. But there are many other aspects that take time to discern.

You can find a diversity of people in most cities, but the predominant mood makes a difference to your daily life and can influence your outlook. The local culture is related to many other criteria; for example, fit and active people tend towards areas rich in outdoor recreation, and career-oriented people are more common in places with high-paying jobs.

To some extent, a local culture is something to learn about and adjust to after moving there. If you're moving from a small town, a large city might have a more stressful work environment, and the reverse move could at first seem too slow-paced for you. On the other hand, moving to a culture that's a better fit for your personality can be invigorating.

Key Information

Here are suggestions on different ways to look at a culture, many of which relate or overlap. Some of this information is available from Census data, by asking people, or best—by visiting. It can take years to really understand a local culture.

- **Tolerance**: How tolerant and accepting are people of others? What's valued more highly—independence and creativity, or conformity and tradition?

- **Family values**: The term "family values" can mean different things, including support for the idea of a nuclear family, protection of children, acceptance of others, or social programs for families in need. How do you define family values and how important are they to you?

- **Recreation:** Are there annual rituals, festivals, or activities that people commonly participate in? Does the town gather for Friday night football games, do most people go to church on Sunday morning, do people drink at the pub after work, are there summer block parties?

- **Heroes:** Does the town have statues of sports stars, business barons, or civil rights advocates? Are there streets named after military veterans, political figures, or early settlers?

- **Cuisine:** The restaurants and types of cooking that people enjoy vary substantially across the country. Look into the local restaurants, scout out the grocery stores, and ask the locals what foods are available.

- **Aesthetics:** Look into what people wear in public, what music they listen to, what movies or TV shows they like to watch, and how they decorate their homes or cars. Do the locals wear tie-dye, hoodies, overalls, or suits? Some areas are more creative and expressive than others: how much of a factor is this?

- **Community:** Do neighborhoods have a feeling of community? Do people watch out for each other?

- **Work culture:** While office cultures vary between industries and types of employers, work culture needs to fit your work style preference. Anywhere you interview, observe what you can of the predominant culture; is it process-based, work hard/play hard, collaborative, male-dominated, or hierarchical?

- **Social conventions:** Are people chatty, aloof, or loud? Are children and pets well-behaved in public? Are the local people friendly and genuine?

- **Social structure:** Is there a big class division between haves and have-nots? Are there pockets of different ethnic groups? Is the culture focused on family life, activities for young singles, or the leisure of being retired?

- **Gender roles:** It might be important to you to be in an area where men and women are treated equally and where women can have fair access to educational or job opportunities. What types of jobs do men and women have? Are there women in local positions of power? How do people split up responsibilities at home for housework, decision-making, and child care?

- **Political attitudes:** How does the area lean politically? Do you want to be exposed to alternative ways of thinking or to be surrounded by people with perspectives similar to yours? Political views can include personal and societal matters like same-sex marriage and abortion as well as economic issues like minimum wage laws and workers' unions.

- **Political engagement:** Are locals informed and involved in local issues? Do residents enter the public debate or are they apathetic? What is the political process is like? Are there town hall meetings where people can speak up (and does anyone listen or are decisions always made behind closed doors)? Do powerful business interests or special interest groups run the show (and are they ethical)?

- **Environmentalism:** Living in a place that encourages sensitive environmental stewardship is desirable for many people. The local environmentalist culture might be reflected in whether recycle bins are available in public areas, if grocers charge for single-use plastic bags, or if there are statutes against Styrofoam take-out containers.

Demographics

Living in a city where you're a demographic minority—maybe the only person in your 20s in an area of families with children or the only black person in a predominantly white town—can be unsettling or an obstacle to making friends. If you're from a minority of any type—ethnic, political, religious, etc.,—moving could be an opportunity to find a place that's a better fit for you.

However, don't rely on stereotypes. For example, suburbs are not always more homogeneous than cities; cities can be gentrified with young professionals and suburbs can be melting pots of immigrants. The Census compiles information on demographics that you can use to identify where there are people similar to you.

Key Information

- **Ethnicity:** People of the same ethnicity have a shared history and often share values. Would you be comfortable in an area where you are part of a small minority, or where there is little ethnic diversity?

- **Age:** Do you want an area with all ages of people or primarily people the same generation as you? An average age can be misleading, as areas with families with children will have a lower average age than areas with singles in their 20s and 30s. Check out a site like the

following for more information:
datatools.metrotrends.org/charts/metrodata/Dashboard/v2/

- **Religion**: What religions are most common? Information on predominant religions is available from the U.S. Census' American Community Survey, which is presented in websites in the Online Resources section at the end of the book.

- **Same-sex households**: Some areas are more accommodating to same-sex partnerships than others. The Census tabulates the number of same-sex couples who live together by state: www.census.gov/prod/2011pubs/acsbr10-03.pdf.

• • •

If you haven't already done it, write down the criteria that are most important to you in the Worksheet: Criteria. Consider all the suggested criteria as well as anything else that's important to you. Decide what you'd be willing to live without and what you must have in your new area.

4 Gather Information

Even if you have a strong idea of where you want to move to, gathering more information can help validate or correct your preconceptions and stereotypes before deciding to relocate.

This process involves gathering a lot of information. As you learn about your prospective cities, you can compile information about them in different ways. Bookmark relevant websites, copy information into another document, write down your own notes in a notebook or on sticky notes, use an online note-taking service, or create a spreadsheet.

If you're still in the process of narrowing down your options, you might use pins on a large map to mark the places you are considering. Add pins as you discover new places, and remove pins from places that no longer fit the bill.

To help you with this process, here are some resources for information, tips to help you make sense of the information you gather, and guidance for visiting a new place.

IDENTIFYING YOUR SAMPLE SIZE

Be aware that you may not have to move far to get what you're looking for, especially in a metropolitan area. Your city may have a strong majority culture that doesn't fit you well, but you might find what you're looking for hidden away in a pocket of the urban fabric. The historic and stately West Village District in Detroit, the hip and progressive Near Southside in Fort Worth, and the low-density, drivable neighborhood of Laurelton in Queens, New York all defy the characteristics of the larger areas where they exist.

Decision-Making Approaches

There are two basic decision-making strategies—optimizing and "satisficing." If you choose the best possible option from among them all, then you're optimizing. If you're willing to move to the first city you find that meets your basic criteria, then you're satisficing. This word is a combination of "satisfying" and "sufficing," coined by Professor Herbert A. Simon in 1956.

For example, if you've been to Sacramento and now you want to move there, that's a satisficing choice. Maybe it's not worth the trouble to study, read about, and visit other cities if you have already found one you like.

If you're an optimizer, you want to make the best choice you can, and it's worth your time to study the whole array of options to confirm what you like. The U.S. Census counts nearly 20,000 incorporated towns in the United States (U.S. Census 2011). And, you might not want to limit your options to those within the country; people often look outside of the country for a more tropical climate, a lower cost of living, or exposure to other cultures. If you're looking globally, there are over 500 cities with more than a million people (Brinkhoff 2014) and hundreds of thousands if you include smaller-sized towns.

With so many options, how do you choose the right one to live in?

Selecting Places

Satisficers might have a place or two in mind already. Longing for lazy days in Laredo? Desiring dreamy sunsets in Destin? Yearning for yachting in Yachats? How about considering only those cities that have a branch office you could transfer to, or those cities where family members live?

If you're seeking an optimal outcome, you start with a large list and narrow down your options by using the process of elimination. For example, if one of your "must have" criteria is to live in a large city, then that eliminates all small towns. If you know you want a cool climate, then you can rule out all areas in warmer climates. Apply the criteria you developed in the previous chapter, and review the following information sources to help you narrow down your list.

> My Experience
>
> *When we first started talking about moving somewhere, we spent a lot of time pondering where we wanted to move to. A lot of analysis went into choosing Seattle.*
>
> *At the time, we knew we were bored with the Dallas/Fort Worth Metroplex and wanted to live somewhere different, but we didn't really have any preconceptions about where we'd like to live.*
>
> *We were optimizers and gathered statistics on 46 large U.S. cities related to the criteria we identified. After we analyzed the data in one big spreadsheet, we decided the top two options for us were Seattle and Portland.*

INFORMATION SOURCES

Trying to decide whether to move to a place you've never been to or only briefly visited can be difficult. However, in today's information age, it's easier than ever to learn about a place from afar.

We've already talked about resources for researching specific aspects of an area and there are additional links in the Online Resources section at the end of the book. Here are a few more places to look for less quantifiable information. Bookmark this page, as these can be useful not only in finding a city to move to, but also in evaluating neighborhoods and other aspects of your destination:

- **Word of mouth:** Talk to people who have visited any of the cities you are interested in and get their opinions. If you have friends (or friends of friends) in the area, ask them about the best areas of town to live in, what people do on the weekends there, or how much the typical rent is. Take advantage of your online social networks to get information too. Ask specific questions about things you don't know that relate to your interests or concerns.

- **Local newspaper:** Reading the local papers, including the daily newspaper, alternative weekly paper, or monthly neighborhood publication can show what the current issues are there. Are the stories about local high school football or gang shootings? Are local politics centered around transportation, jobs, or scandal?

- **Local blogs:** Searching the web for blogs in your city should turn up dozens. Between sports blogs, blogs about particular neighborhoods, or personal blogs from residents—you can glean local perspectives.

- **Message boards:** There are several Internet forums about choosing a city, such as City-Data.com. You can read what other people have to say or ask questions to address any of your concerns.

- **Social media:** Search for local news sources or restaurants to follow on Twitter to get local recommendations and a feel for the vibe of the city.

- **Look at photos of a place:** Search online for photos of your city to see what people take pictures of. Look at city streets on Google Street View to give you a feel for the different parts of town.

- **Newcomer's guide:** Look for a mover's guide or newcomer's guide to your city, either in book or website form.

- **Travel literature:** Know that a good place to visit isn't the same as a good place to live. While you may enjoy tourist activities during your first year of residence in your new home, you'll probably only visit them again when visitors come. However, travel books can give you a feel for what there is to do there—pointing out interesting neighborhoods and identifying which beaches are better for surfing or sunbathing. Try the city's local convention and visitors bureau, other travel websites, or books at the library to learn more about the place.

- **Government websites:** Your town and state will have their own websites with information on local public services like parks, schools, and police; information on taxes and laws; and links to local cultural and social organizations. Once you have chosen your destination, these websites will be useful resources for information on things like vehicle registration, purchasing a home, volunteer opportunities, and community events.

- **Chamber of Commerce:** Some cities will send you books and maps for free if you register an interest in living there. The chamber of commerce is a primary resource for information on doing business, including incentives, laws, organizations, and activities.

- **Others who have moved:** Talk to people who have moved before and find out what they've learned. The more their situation matches yours in age, destination, or motivation, the more relevant their experience will be to you. They might help you avoid making their mistakes or provide insight on additional references.

- **Visit:** The most insightful way to learn about a place, but also the most expensive, is to visit. This is covered fully later in this chapter.

INFORMATION CAVEATS

There is a lot of available information, but resist taking any one piece of information too seriously. It's best to take multiple sources of information under advisement. You're making a significant, life-changing decision, and scanty or unreliable data could lead you astray. Here are some specific things to watch out for as you study the available information.

Misconceptions

There are many stereotypes about cities: it rains all the time in Seattle (false, summer is quite dry); LA is always sunny (false, it rains almost four inches per month in winter); and everyone in Oklahoma experiences tornadoes regularly (false, tornadoes are very localized weather phenomena). There may be a grain of truth in the stereotypes, but look into the information for yourself.

Be careful when someone is telling you about a place; people's perceptions are notoriously inaccurate and biased. People tend to boast about their hometowns and most people's memory of a place can be colored by whatever inner experience they were having at the time.

Second-hand information can still be very valuable, but choosing your new home deserves more than just someone else's opinion.

Rankings

The web is littered with "The Best Cities for Jobs," "Top Places to Raise a Family," "America's Fittest Cities," and numerous other city rankings to tell you exactly where to move, given the life situation you're in or the lifestyle you're looking for.

While these lists sometimes look as if they were written just for you, they're not. The criteria used to make these lists are likely different than what you would include, and are often too limited to provide good guidance, unless a city's fitness, for example, is the only thing that matters to you.

That's not to say that these lists are worthless; reading them can be fun and even helpful. They do provide a glimpse of each city on the list, and if you regularly see the same few cities on lists, then you might want to pay special attention to those places.

Statistics

Lots of statistics are available on cities, counties, and states. You can look up how your county voted in the last election, how much your state funds K-12 education, or what the unemployment rate is in your city. Statistics can be misleading, however.

Statistics provide an element of information but lack the details you need in order to relate those statistics to your life. So when looking at statistics for an area, you'll probably want to compare them to statistics for the area where you live now in order to have a reference point.

Also, realize that statistics are skewed by arbitrary city or state borders. When you think of your "hometown," the boundaries in your mind are probably different than the actual physical city limits. So, when you look at statistics about your city, the area being included doesn't exactly match the area that you think of as part of your hometown. There are probably parts of the city you live in today that you never visit and may not even be aware of. If you find that a city is indicated as dangerous, could that be because of some areas on one side of town where most of the crime occurs? Or if a city is known for its bad traffic, could that be an issue that affects only specific roadways at certain times?

Taking It All into Account

So, if none of the sources are completely trustworthy, what can you trust?

The short answer is, you can't trust any piece of information by itself. The tourist information might be too promising, the residents might be too discouraging, and the stereotypes could be completely outdated.

Synthesize the information you've gathered; the more information that says the same thing, the more likely it's true.

The next chapter talks about ways in which you can make a decision on a place to live and look at either as much or as little information as needed to make your best decision.

VISITING

If you can narrow your list down to three or fewer options, visiting those cities is a good idea before choosing one to relocate to. Be serious about developing your criteria before choosing a place to visit. If you don't have a short list of places, we'll talk later about some ways to narrow down your options.

Simply visiting a place for a few days to explore it firsthand will provide you with a feel for the place and a better understanding of whether it may be right for you. You have a unique perspective on things, so you will construe a place differently from anyone else. For instance, what appears to be a vibrant urban neighborhood to one person might look run-down and unsafe to someone else. What one person perceives as plentiful retail and bargain shopping may well look like unappealing suburban sprawl to someone else.

Planning Your Visit

When you're visiting a place to determine whether you want to live there, it's not a vacation; think of it as a personal business trip. You're going there to experience things that you can't discover from afar, to understand the personalities behind the stereotypes, and to imagine what it would be like if you woke up there every day.

To get a better perspective, spread your visit over two or three days that include both a weekend and a weekday. A downtown that's busy on a weekday may be deserted on a weekend. Or a roadway that you had all to yourself on Sunday afternoon may be clogged with traffic during the Monday morning commute.

Before you go, use the Worksheet: Pre-Visit Prep to make a list of preconceptions (either positive or negative) that you'll want to check and questions that you want answers to.

Reach out to any contacts in your new city during your preliminary visits, such as relatives, friends, colleagues, or business contacts. Let them know why you're visiting and try to arrange to meet them to ask questions and gather more information.

You might want to take your children with you, especially if you plan to involve them in the decision-making. If nothing else, bringing them for a visit should make it easier for your children to be prepared if your family does end up relocating there.

After your initial visit, you may need to return a few more times for job interviews and to look for housing. You can save time and money by achieving multiple objectives on a single visit, so before buying plane tickets, consider what else you want to accomplish while you're there. You'll also want to keep an eye on costs so that you have enough money for the actual move, even after any visits to places you're considering. (We'll talk about budgets, later.)

WORKSHEET: PRE-VISIT PREP

Before visiting your potential new home, identify as clearly as possible any preconceptions that you can validate (or correct) and questions you can answer. Look into each preconception and question and write down what you find out. Complete this worksheet for each place you're seriously considering, regardless of whether you are able to visit.

Place:_____

Dates Visited: _____

Here are things I think about the place I'm visiting—I'll try to find out if these are true:

> e.g., Preconception: Traffic is terrible;
> What I found: Rush hour traffic is heavy in some areas

1. Preconception _____

   What I found:_____

2. Preconception _____

   What I found:_____

3. Preconception _____

   What I found:_____

4. Preconception _____

   What I found:_____

5. Preconception _____

   What I found:_____

6. Preconception _____

   What I found:_____

7. Preconception _____

   What I found:_____

Here are questions I have about the place I'm visiting—I'll try to answer these:

e.g., How much does a three-bedroom, two-bath home there cost?
What I found: There are many options from $200,000 to $240,000

1. Question: _____

   What I found _____

2. Question: _____

   What I found _____

3. Question: _____

   What I found _____

4. Question: _____

   What I found _____

5. Question: _____

   What I found _____

6. Question: _____

   What I found _____

7. Question: _____

   What I found _____

What to Look For

When you're there, skip the Empire State Building, the Space Needle, or the giant Popsicle tower. If you move there, you can do all that stuff later. Just in case you don't end up moving there, you could set aside an afternoon to do some sightseeing, but you want to spend as much time as possible putting yourself in the shoes of a local.

Plan your trip based on the criteria you identified earlier and the items you identified in the Worksheet: Pre-Visit Prep. When you're there, take notes and record your thoughts.

Spend sufficient time in areas you might want to live in. Visiting different neighborhoods will help you gain a sense for the variety of subcultures within the city.

You'll also want to engage with local people. Search online in advance or pick up a copy of the newspaper when you arrive to see if there are any festivals, plays, or other cultural events going on that would give you a glimpse into the culture and lifestyle of the people. Talk to cashiers at the grocery store and waiters at restaurants. Seek out opportunities to converse with others, even just to ask for directions. Observe people to see if you would be comfortable among them. How do they behave, talk, and dress?

Imagine what your daily life would be like. Is there a homey coffee shop just around the corner? Are there a variety of local stores? Is getting around difficult either due to traffic, difficult drivers, or inadequate public transit?

Be aware of the season you're visiting in. Is the town buried in snow during winter? Does everyone stay inside during the dog days of summer? Ask a local if the weather you're experiencing is normal.

Weigh how a city feels in comparison to your hometown. Another idea is to hire a taxi or car service to take you around so you can focus on looking out the window rather than driving or navigating.

Don't let a single experience change how you feel about a place. Walking by a flower stand on a sunny day can make anywhere seem vibrant and beautiful. On the other hand, don't let a bad experience at a hotel and being caught in a thunderstorm with no umbrella ruin your perspective.

My Experience

During our first visit to Seattle, we wanted to get a sense of how good the public transportation was, so we made a point to travel everywhere by bus. We saw some tourist attractions, but we also visited neighborhoods we were interested in as well as parks that we expected to enjoy after moving.

We enjoyed mostly sunny skies during that visit. When we went back to Seattle for job interviews and to look for homes, we went in January. Then we tried to get a sense of whether we could effectively endure the rain that Seattle is known for.

What Have You Learned?

What are your overall feelings from your visit? Were you energized or exhausted by the place? Intrigued or bored? Homesick or right at home?

Complete the Worksheet: Pre-Visit Prep with your findings. Review your observations and write about your experience in the Worksheet: Post-Visit Evaluation. While visiting won't tell you exactly how much you'll like a place once you move there, your impressions from a couple days' visit should go a long way towards helping you compare options.

WORKSHEET: POST-VISIT EVALUATION

After visiting a location that you like, fill out this worksheet.

Place:_____

Dates Visited: _____

- My favorite part of town was:

  _____

  _____

- My least favorite part of town was:

  _____

  _____

- The people seemed:

  _____

  _____

- The weather was:

  _____

  _____

- When I was there, I felt:

  _____

  _____

- The most surprising thing was:

  _____

  _____

- The most pleasant sight was:

  _____

  _____

- The most concerning thing was:

  _____

  _____

- My biggest concerns about living there would be:

  _____

  _____

- The most appealing aspect about living there would be:

  _____

  _____

- These are some of the key differences from what I'm used to:

  o _____

     Could I get used to this? Circle one: Yes No Maybe

  o _____

     Could I get used to this? Circle one: Yes No Maybe

  o _____

     Could I get used to this? Circle one: Yes No Maybe

  o _____

     Could I get used to this? Circle one: Yes No Maybe

  o _____

     Could I get used to this? Circle one: Yes No Maybe

Also consider the other information sources you've reviewed. Is any one place a clear frontrunner or do you need to spend more time evaluating your options?

• • •

You could continue gathering information about a place indefinitely, but after researching and visiting, there will come a time when you have enough information to make a decision.

5 Evaluate and Decide

Once you've determined your criteria, identified your places, and possibly even visited one or two, you'll have to decide whether you like the new places more than where you live now and where you'll make your home.

DECISION FRAMEWORK

Here are a few decision-making techniques you can use to narrow down your options and decide between your top choices.

Before you rack your brain trying to decide, first set up a framework for your decision-making. Even if you don't have all the answers to plug in now, be aware that an approach along these lines can be helpful.

1. Define your options. Is the choice between staying in your current home or relocating to a future home in a place you've already chosen? Or do you want to move and are choosing where to go from a short list of options?

2. Contemplate how long you would be moving for. If later, your move seems like a mistake, how soon could you come back or go

somewhere else? If you can relocate again relatively easily, are you more open to a risky option? Or are you planning to relocate and then stay put?

3. Think about what the tiebreaker will be between close options and whether other influences play in. Do you automatically choose the place that best meets the criteria you established earlier? Do you want the choice that excites you the most or the most comfortable choice? Is your current place the default option unless you're completely convinced that there's something better?

If you're overwhelmed by the decision, simplify your approach. Looking at too much information can result in "information overload" or "analysis paralysis." If that happens, just focus on what's really important to you based on the criteria you've set. Try not to get bogged down in trying to make sense of every detail.

TOOLS FOR DECIDING

There are many ways to come to a decision. Some, you can just do in your head; others are more involved, so worksheets can help you organize your thoughts. You might want to involve the other people who will be moving with you or perhaps ask a friend who can be a good sounding board. In any case, feel free to use the tools that make the most sense to you and ignore the rest.

Listening to Your Gut

Making a quick gut decision can in some cases be the right one, especially if you understand your options very well. If you have a gut reaction that tells you what you're leaning towards, you can think about it more to see if that still seems like the right answer. This approach can take some pressure off and simplify the decision-making process by giving you a preferred option.

Looking at Your Criteria

Process of Elimination

Once you have gathered information on your top places, look for ways to eliminate more options.

Maybe a city on your list doesn't satisfy one of your "must have" criteria or has some very negative aspects. One city on your list may seem like the perfect place but is outside of your budget.

Original Criteria

Whether you have two options or twenty, comparing your options to your original criteria can lead you to a single answer. This can be done using the Worksheet: Criteria Evaluation, which you can fill in with your criteria plus your evaluations of certain places. This approach allows you to quantify how you see things.

> MY EXPERIENCE
>
> *This is the approach we used, although neither Seattle nor Portland were actually the top outcome of this exercise. There were other places whose total score was higher. However, those places had fairly substantial drawbacks. We chose Seattle because it had the fewest aspects that we felt were unsatisfactory.*

WORKSHEET: CRITERIA EVALUATION

Rate the options to compare them in terms of the top criteria you identified earlier.

1. List your criteria from Chapter 3 in the *Criteria* column.

2. Assign a weight in the *Weight* column for each criterion based on how you prioritized them earlier:

   For "must-haves" or "must-not-haves," assign a weight of 10

   For "should-haves," assign a weight of 4

   For "nice-to-haves," assign a weight of 1

3. Write the names of the places you're considering moving to in the top row boxes that say "Place A," "Place B," etc.,

4. This part is where your research comes in. For each place you've identified, go down the list of criteria and write in a numerical rating:

   exceeds expectations = 2

   meets expectations = 1

   acceptable = 0

   unsatisfactory = -1

5. Once your sheet is completely full of criteria and numbers, then you can use the numbers to determine total scores. Go row by row and multiply the weight of each criterion by the rating you've entered. Then add up all these numbers for each location.

6. The place with the highest score is the one that best meets your criteria. If there are close competitors, follow other suggested decision-making exercises to validate your top choice.

CRITERIA	WEIGHT	PLACE A	PLACE B
1.			
2.			
3.			
4.			
5.			
6.			
7.			
8.			
9.			
10.			
11.			
12.			
13.			
14.			
15.			
16.			
17.			
18.			
19.			
20.			
21.			
22.			
23.			
24.			
TOTAL SCORES			

Exploring the Good and Bad

Pros and Cons

Listing pros and cons is a simple and time-tested way of making decisions. Use a page of the Worksheet: Pros and Cons for each option you're considering and list the positives of that choice on one side and the minuses on the other. Sometimes, just listing the pros and cons can give you a clearer sense of which option is best.

WORKSHEET: PROS AND CONS

Write down the pros and cons for one location at a time.

Place:_____

Pros   **Cons**

_____   _____

_____   _____

_____   _____

_____   _____

_____   _____

_____   _____

_____   _____

_____   _____

_____   _____

_____   _____

_____   _____

_____   _____

_____   _____

Total Count:

_____   _____

To take your list of pros and cons to a more advanced level, here are some things you can do:

- Count the total pros and the total minuses and see which option has the largest advantage of pluses to minuses.

- A variant of this is called PMI, for "Plus, Minus, Interesting." You add a third column labeled "Interesting" where you list possible outcomes that may or may not happen and could be good or bad.

- Assign a weight to each item in your list—from 1 (unimportant) to 5 (extremely important)—and add up the score of each column to identify which one is more persuasive.

- Based on the weights you've assigned, identify the most significant benefit and the most significant detriment of each option. Ask yourself if the biggest benefit outweighs the worst downside.

- Write an essay to try to sell yourself on each option you're considering by featuring the pros from your list.

Deconstruct Your Concerns

It can be hard to even face a decision like this if you have a fear of the unknown and see a series of major obstacles in your way. Be careful about fear; don't let it control your decisions. If you're concerned about moving or aren't sure, try to look at your specific concerns in more detail. Fears can take the form of cons in your "Pros and Cons" list.

Use the Worksheet: Deconstruct Concerns to list your top concerns, and then try to think about ways to handle each of them. Can you tell how valid they are?

If you're not sure that you can live with some of the concerns you have, research the facts. Is there anything you can do to investigate or eliminate those fears? If you see an obstacle, talk it over with people. There could be a solution you hadn't thought of; maybe your new school will give you some transfer credits, maybe your aging mother is willing to move with you, or maybe you could keep your current job and just work from home. Talk to others or look inside yourself to determine whether you can successfully get past your fears.

WORKSHEET: DECONSTRUCT CONCERNS

This worksheet can help you sort through your fears in the early stages of considering a move or if you're trying to make a final decision on where to live.

Concerns	Possible ways to validate and address concerns
e.g., The job market is tough	*I will be sure to get a job there before I move*
e.g., I won't fit in	*I will visit beforehand and talk to people*
e.g., Homes are too expensive	*I will look into actual costs with a roommate*

1. Concern_____

    Ways to validate and address concern _____

    _____

    _____

2. Concern_____

    Ways to validate and address concern _____

    _____

    _____

3. Concern_____

    Ways to validate and address concern _____

    _____

    _____

4. Concern_____

    Ways to validate and address concern _____

    _____

    _____

5. Concern_____

    Ways to validate and address concern _____

    _____

    _____

6. Concern_____

    Ways to validate and address concern _____

    _____

    _____

7. Concern_____

    Ways to validate and address concern _____

    _____

    _____

8. Concern_____

    Ways to validate and address concern _____

    _____

    _____

Opportunity Cost

One factor you can account for in your decision is the opportunity cost. That is, what is the cost to you of not choosing the other option?

For example, if you're choosing between staying where you are and moving away, an opportunity cost of moving could include "not being able to spend time with my friends here," "not being able to enjoy my favorite restaurants here," and "missing my family (here) on the holidays."

On the other hand, the opportunity costs of staying could be thoughts like, "I'll miss the adventure of discovering a new place," "I'll miss the chance to outfit my own apartment," or "I won't be able to room with my best friend on the other side of the country."

Write down the opportunity costs for each place in the Worksheet: Opportunity Costs. Are there any costs you are not willing to pay? Do the costs of one option exceed the costs of another? Follow some of the suggested practices in the Pros and Cons process to evaluate this list.

WORKSHEET: OPPORTUNITY COSTS

Opportunity costs for Place A	Opportunity costs for Place B
_____	_____
_____	_____
_____	_____
_____	_____
_____	_____
_____	_____
_____	_____
_____	_____
_____	_____

Total Count:

_____   _____

Six Thinking Hats

This is a method popularized in the book of the same name by Edward de Bono. In this decision-making process, you examine the decision from different angles, each represented by a different-colored hat:

- **Information (white hat)**: Look at just the facts available to you, including statistics and other information you've gathered.

- **Emotions (red hat)**: Weigh the matter from an emotional perspective, using an instinctive gut reaction and emotions.

- **Discernment (black hat)**: Look carefully at your options and analyze why each option might not be a good option. This perspective can help you identify any drawbacks, make contingency plans, and take a cautious approach.

- **Optimistic (yellow hat)**: Look at the benefits of each option.

- **Creativity (green):** Look at your options in a creative way. If there are drawbacks to one option, wear this hat to find creative potential solutions. You might even discover additional options while wearing this hat.

- **Process (blue):** This hat guides the exercise and helps you move through the process effectively. Put the blue hat on after each other hat to identify what hat to wear next, or if you should wear any other hats yet one more time to explore that perspective more completely.

External and Internal Influences

Influence from Others

Talk about your options with someone. Have tea with your grandmother, text your buddy, or chat with a stranger. Just start sharing your thoughts and see if talking your options through with others helps make things clearer or if other people's opinions help you think it through. This can be a very powerful way to reach a decision.

Impacts to Others

Consider people, like parents, who will be affected by your decision. Some people feel a sense of duty to respect the path their elders have laid before them, while others might feel entitled to decide by themselves how to live their own life. Regardless, understanding the impact of your decision on others could be part of a pros and cons list and play into your decision.

Influence from Meditation or Spirituality

Look deep inside yourself through meditation or look towards the heavens for guidance from a higher power. Participating in regular meditation can clarify your thoughts, steady you in transition, and help with making this decision. Saying evening prayers or reflecting on spiritual teachings can influence your thoughts and decisions.

Creating a Vision for Your Life

Life Vision Exercise

Another way to help you align where you live with your goals in life is to clarify your vision for your life. This exercise is adapted from the book *Success Principles* by Jack Canfield. By envisioning your desired lifestyle, writing it down, and even sharing it with others, you'll be more likely to achieve that vision. Exploring your vision can help you compare among your alternatives.

Review the following topics and ask yourself what you envision as the *ideal status* for each aspect of your life. As you answer these, try to imagine answers to any related questions and use plenty of description to paint a mental picture of your life. You could also literally paint a picture of your vision.

- **Career:** What is your career? Where do you work? Whom do you work with?

- **Recreation:** What do you do for fun? Do you have free time? Do you pursue any hobbies?

- **Physical:** What is your vision of your body? How much do you weigh? Do you exercise? What do you eat? What is your mindset and mood?

- **Relationships:** What are your relationships like with other people? Do you have many friends? Are you close to family? Are you in a committed relationship? What kinds of things do you do with other people?

- **Personal:** Are you pursuing more education? Are you involved in a spiritual community? Do you spend time reading?

- **Financial:** How much income do you make? How much do you have saved? What material possessions do you have? What kind of home do you live in?

- **Community:** What kind of community do you live in? How do people treat each other? What kinds of activities take place? Are there charitable events? If so, what do they benefit?

Review your responses to these. Now imagine living in each of the places you are considering; express your vision for what your life would be like in each locale. How would your vision be affected by each place? Which option supports the most important aspects of your vision?

> MY EXPERIENCE
>
> *For us, the move was something we explored and became more and more intent on as we thought about it. The more we looked at it from the perspective that "maybe we could move," the more support we found for that decision.*
>
> *We knew we wanted to move to Seattle or Portland, but Lesley and I couldn't decide between them even after visiting. Actually, we did know what we wanted, but we each wanted different things. We tried working through the decision together but couldn't.*
>
> *So, we decided that we would move to the place that offered one of us a job. We both looked for jobs in both places, but eventually Lesley got a job offer in Seattle. And that broke the tie for us.*

OTHER OPTIONS

Choosing an Alternative

If you have a hard time saying yes to moving but don't want to say no, you could choose something in between.

If you can afford it, you could travel for a few weeks to gain perspective on the world.

You could try a temporary move. If you like a particular place but aren't ready for a commitment, maybe you can travel to your destination and stay for a while, especially if you have the ability to work anywhere or can save money by staying with a friend. Use Vacation Rentals by Owner or Airbnb to save money and have a more authentic local experience than you would at a hotel.

Deciding Not to Move After All

If you decide not to move, having gone through this process has helped you to better understand yourself.

Your final decision will have to depend on your personal preferences and abilities. If you don't move to your dream city, there might be some way to seek the elements in your current city that are more like the place you want to be, or you could add your prospective cities to your vacation plans.

Or perhaps you are fortunate and are already in the right place for you.

STEPPING BACK

Here are some final suggestions in case you're still having trouble making a decision.

If you can't decide after looking over the statistics, visiting a place, and asking friends, set the topic aside for a few days and try not to worry too much about it. During that time, your subconscious will synthesize the information so that when you revisit the question of whether to move, the tension will have lessened and the decision might come more easily for you.

Try to mentally step back from the decision you're facing and put your life in perspective. Usually, the younger you are, the more of life you have ahead of you. It's easy to be shortsighted in a decision. Imagine yourself 5, 10, 20, or 50 years from now—how would you look back at this decision?

Weighing the Options

If you're struggling to decide between two options and the arguments for both places are too persuasive, it could mean that *you can't really make a bad decision.* Perhaps both options are quite good. Also, realize that there is no perfect answer in life.

There is something to be said about familiarity. You may already be in a place where you are comfortable and have a network of family, friends, and acquaintances. If being away from them doesn't excite you much, then maybe it's worth staying where you are. At some point, the reasons for moving could be more compelling and you could relocate then.

On the other hand, you don't want to regret not having the courage to try something you wish you had. You may never have a completely perfect opportunity to move. There will always be valid reasons not to move—so don't wait for perfection.

• • •

While each option leads you in a different direction, you can't know which one will be better down the road. Sometimes all you can do is try to make the decision that seems right for you now and hope for the best.

Even if you're not completely confident in a decision, continuing to read through this book will help you explore what moving would be like and to better assess if it's the best choice for you. If you *are* planning to move, let's figure out how to sort through all the details in order to make it happen.

PREPARING TO RELOCATE

6 Plan

Unless you're going to start driving to your destination tomorrow, there's probably a lot that you need to do to make your dream home real. As French aviator and author Antoine de Saint-Exupéry said, "A goal without a plan is just a wish."

A great first step is to create a plan that prepares you to cope with changes, reduce stress, and increase your success.

SETTING A SUCCESSFUL MINDSET

Acknowledge Your Emotions

After you have made the decision to move, you might experience emotions ranging from excitement to anxiety, fear, sadness, and depression. You now have the chance for new experiences, but you also have to leave your familiar home behind.

While there are myriad reasons to look forward to a move, many people dread moving. Packing boxes isn't normally what people like to do with their time. There are also the emotional aspects of moving—saying goodbye to the place that has been your home, along with all of the memories and people who have been part of that home. Leaving an old home can put you through a process similar to grieving over someone's death, no matter how positive the circumstances surrounding your move.

Moving is a major change that can disrupt your life, make it hard to sleep, cause you to overeat, and slim your wallet. But the way you prepare yourself for the move can make a huge difference.

To help you acknowledge and process your emotions, try writing down some of your feelings in the Worksheet: Acknowledge Your Emotions.

WORKSHEET: ACKNOWLEDGE YOUR EMOTIONS

Things I'm worried about   **I'm worried because**

_____   _____

_____   _____

_____   _____

_____   _____

_____   _____

_____   _____

_____   _____

Things I'm excited about   **I'm excited because**

_____   _____

_____   _____

_____   _____

_____   _____

_____   _____

_____   _____

_____   _____

Coping Techniques

Change is uncomfortable, but here are some suggestions to keep the big picture in mind, cope with the challenges, and stay upbeat after you decide to make this major life change:

- **Maintain your habits:** Spending every night looking for jobs or packing boxes is stressful. If you used to go to the gym after work or play poker with friends on Fridays, keep those habits up. While you could spend that time working on relocating, it's not helpful to become so singularly focused on moving that you're miserable.

- **Be methodical:** You can't do it all at once. Trying to can cause anxiety, and overdoing it can cause mistakes, accidents, and further delay.

- **Find someone to talk to:** Stay in close contact with a friend with whom you can chat about your move. You can also hire a relocation consultant, therapist, or coach before you get into the thick of the move so you know you'll have a supportive professional throughout and even after the process.

- **Explore your feelings:** Understand what's causing your stress and anxiety. Are you afraid of how you'll adjust to your new place? Do you have some business to finish before you leave? Are you sad to be leaving good memories behind? Do you regret how things have gone where you are?

- **Don't let your thoughts keep you awake:** If you tend to think of things you need to do as you're trying to go to sleep, put a pen and paper by the bed so that you can quickly jot down any thoughts that occur and review them the next day.

- **Record your experience:** As you prepare for the move, start a journal, blog, or scrapbook to keep track of your thoughts and experiences.

- **Exercise:** Start going to the gym again to get your blood flowing. Studies show that just a little exercise—even if it's just a walk around the block—can elevate your mood.

- **Prayer:** If it applies to you, deepen your faith and increase your prayer regimen to keep your mind clear.

- **Have confidence:** If thousands of other people can do this—many of whom don't have a guide book—then you can do it too and do it even better.

> ## My Experience
>
> *Once we made the decision to move, we decided to start a blog to document our thoughts. We shared it with a few close friends and used it to let people know what we were planning. We had a lot to figure out once we decided to relocate, and the blog was a helpful way to share that experience. Writing was also therapeutic and helped us to think through what was going on.*

Feel free to cry when you need to, but keep the big picture in mind: all this work is necessary to achieve a major and positive change in your life. Don't let the stress get to you; take it easy whenever you can. Set aside time to relax and sleep—and have fun!

Anticipating Problems

Prepare yourself for problems during your moving process—you will probably do dumb things. And there are everyday challenges that you'll have to endure. You might be too late to reserve the specific home you want; you could accidentally make a four-hour detour while driving to your new city, or your movers may drop your piano out of the window—cartoons suggest this is quite common.

Things will go wrong, so all you can do is anticipate mishaps as best you can and respond well when they happen. If you tend to be anxious about how things unfold, fill out a "Risk Mitigation Plan." Basically that's a fancy way to think ahead, prepare for things that could pose a risk to the smooth success of your move, and come up with ways to prevent difficulties.

For example, if you're afraid that there could be a blizzard during your move, your contingency plan could be to delay your move by a week until the weather pattern has passed. If you're afraid your mother-in-law could discourage your move, you could suggest that she find her own place somewhere near where you're planning to move.

Think through as many details as you can while making your risk mitigation list. Maybe you're assuming that you'll get a job right after your move, so ask yourself what you would do if you aren't able to find a job quickly. Or, if you're expecting friends to help you move, ask how you would handle it if some of them are out of town on your moving weekend.

You can't predict everything, but by anticipating any obstacles you can think of, you can feel more prepared.

As you think of the scenarios that could occur during your moving process, decide what the impact would be to your move:

- **High:** Would cause you to rethink or abandon your plans to move
- **Medium:** Would disrupt your plans significantly
- **Low:** Would have a minimal effect on your ability to move

Also, estimate what the likelihood is that the feared situation will happen.

- **High:** Likely to happen
- **Medium:** 50/50 chance
- **Low:** Probably won't happen

If you find it helpful, use the Worksheet: Risk Mitigation Plan to work through these possibilities.

As you fill out this worksheet (or do a similar exercise in your head), note any items that would have a high impact on your move and are also highly likely to occur—and put more thought into these particular issues.

As the move proceeds, update this list as risks drop off and you discover new ones.

WORKSHEET: RISK MITIGATION PLAN

Write down all your fears and how you would address them.

What could go wrong	Impact	Likelihood	How I can respond
	H M L	H M L	
_____	☐☐☐	☐☐☐	_____
_____	☐☐☐	☐☐☐	_____
_____	☐☐☐	☐☐☐	_____
_____	☐☐☐	☐☐☐	_____
_____	☐☐☐	☐☐☐	_____
_____	☐☐☐	☐☐☐	_____
_____	☐☐☐	☐☐☐	_____
_____	☐☐☐	☐☐☐	_____
_____	☐☐☐	☐☐☐	_____

Think About the Positive

Like in any part of life, what you focus on will affect the way you experience your relocation process. There are lots of reasons to be excited by the moving process—after all, moving is an adventure.

While many people move because they "have to" for work or family, even these "non-choice" movers can enrich their moving experience by adopting an adventure perspective. Moving somewhere new, even if it's not the place of your dreams, can at least inspire those dreams. It can be helpful to cultivate a feeling that you are "being moved" by fate and that this change is part of your destiny.

During your move, people will likely be more interested in your situation than they normally are, which adds to the positive excitement. Make it fun, and look forward to the exploration and discovery of a new home.

Moving Motivation

Lest the challenges of moving get you down, here are some techniques you can use to maintain your motivation and make headway on moving:

- **Written reminders**: Writing down your goals can help make them more concrete. Make your goal specific, such as: "I will be living large in Laramie, Wyoming before next Christmas." By posting that message in a visible location and regularly rereading it, you'll be bolstering your positive energy.

- **Visual reminders**: Visual cues can tap into instincts that drive action. Put a picture of your future hometown on your wall or as a background image on your computer or phone to remind yourself of where you want to be.

- **Visualize your success**: Athletes and other high performers use creative visualization to help them succeed. Mentally "see" yourself packing your things and then arriving in your new place. Immerse your mind in the idea that you're enjoying long walks on the beach or lattes by the lake near your new home.

- **Assume the world is working with you**: Rather than feeling that everyone is out to prevent you from reaching your goals, take the attitude that everything in the world is working to *help you* reach your goals. Look for the opportunity in every challenge.

Relocating Your Family

If you are moving as part of a family, having a good mindset may be difficult if others are miserable. Often the person who leads the moving is happier than the others being moved. Family members can feel helpless, angry, or resentful if they feel that they're being moved against their wishes.

Help each person in the family understand what will benefit them in the move, but also acknowledge what they're giving up. Even if family members don't have a choice about whether or not to move, it's good to involve them as much as possible. Just remember that involving people while disregarding their opinions can be counterproductive.

Keep in mind that children's stress during a move is lower if children are involved in preparation and parents explain to them what will happen. Write down the steps of the moving process for them and welcome their questions.

Set aside time every week to sit down together and discuss what's happening, how you're all feeling, and what needs to happen next. You can each take time to share your fears and things you're looking forward to. Use those thoughts as a starting point to help validate everyone's concerns and explore their excitement. Remind each other of specific results of the move, whether big or small, that you can all look forward to.

Use the Worksheet: Acknowledge Your Emotions to help you and your family understand your feelings. Talk about what you can do to address your fears now. Then talk about all the things individuals are looking forward to.

If you write these down, you can look back at these after the move. Family members will see their emotional journeys connected with the move and likely feel a great sense of accomplishment. They may even laugh at the things that had frightened them earlier.

As you learn more about your new location and find a new home, share details and photos to help your family align with what's happening and become excited about living there.

Planning to Move

Making a Plan

Let's face it: uprooting your life, saying goodbye to all your friends, and relocating all of your possessions hundreds or thousands of miles—not to mention resettling in a new and unfamiliar place—can be daunting.

The process is made easier if you have a plan to help you stay on track, know what to do next, and keep your goal in mind.

At the heart of it, moving is just a project. Like any other project, this one is made up of a lot of small tasks.

Your project will go much more smoothly if you follow the same techniques that project managers use to build magnificent bridges or create complex software programs. Or conversely, as Ben Franklin said, "By failing to prepare, you are preparing to fail."

While experience and a skilled team of experts is necessary for the biggest feats in industry, you and a few friends or family members can successfully bridge your life across the country.

The first tool you need is a good plan. List all the steps you need to follow in order to move. You'll need to find a place to stay, figure out how to move your stuff, say goodbye to people, and so on. By making a list, you will understand more clearly what you need to do and have the satisfaction of crossing tasks off as you complete them. To help you further, you may want to associate dates, durations, and specific numbers with certain items. For example, "I will start applying for jobs in two weeks and then submit 10 résumés per week until I find a job."

While a detailed plan isn't for everyone, it's certainly an important tool to consider using during your moving process. Here is an example plan, already filled out with steps that line up with the sections of the upcoming chapters.

Example Step-by-Step Plan

	STEP	HOW LONG TO START BEFORE MOVE	DURATION
	EMPLOYMENT		
	Prepare for job search	12–52 weeks	1–4 weeks
1.	Create a plan		
2.	Prepare your résumé		
3.	Build skills and experience		
	Find jobs	12–52 weeks	4–52 weeks
4.	Search for jobs, employers, and connections		
5.	Submit applications or résumés		
	Accept a job	2–8 weeks	2–12 weeks
6.	Interview		
7.	Choose		
8.	Negotiate and accept		
	NEW HOME		
	Prepare for home search	12–26 weeks	1–4 weeks
9.	Create a plan		
10.	Establish your criteria		
	Find homes	8–20 weeks	4–39 weeks
11.	Find and explore neighborhoods		
12.	Visit homes		
13.	Make a decision		
	The transaction	2–8 weeks	1–6 weeks
14.	Apply or submit your offer		
15.	Sign on the dotted line		

	STEP	HOW LONG TO START BEFORE MOVE	DURATION
PLANNING HOW YOU'LL MOVE			
	Possessions	**6–20 weeks**	**1–16 weeks**
16.	Determine how to move your things		
17.	Get estimates from movers		
18.	Schedule move with movers		
	People	**6–20 weeks**	**1–18 weeks**
19.	Decide how to move yourself		
20.	Decide how to move your pets		
21.	Make arrangements		
SAYING GOODBYE			
22.	Sell your home	8–39 weeks	6–39 weeks
23.	Pare down your possessions	12–26 weeks	2–26 weeks
24.	Take care of the details	4–25 weeks	4–25 weeks
25.	Let people know	2–6 weeks	1–6 weeks
THE MOVE			
	Prepare	**3–8 weeks**	**1–4 weeks**
26.	Acquire moving materials		
	Pack	**2–6 weeks**	**2–6 weeks**
27.	Out-of-season clothes and decorations	4–6 weeks	1–3 weeks
28.	Books, movies, games, and other media you don't plan to use	2–6 weeks	1–3 weeks
29.	Any other non-essential items	1–4 weeks	1–4 weeks
30.	Essentials to fit in your suitcase	1–2 weeks	1–2 weeks
31.	Daily use items (e.g., clothes, dishes)	1–2 weeks	1–2 weeks

	STEP	HOW LONG TO START BEFORE MOVE	DURATION
MOVING DAY			
ARRIVE AND MOVE IN			
	Move In		
32.	Unpack and put things away	Immediately	1–8 weeks
	Making Your Home		
33.	Decorate and purchase housewares	Immediately	1–4 weeks
34.	Prepare for safety	Immediately	1 week

WORKSHEET: YOUR PLAN

Fill in this template to help you plan your move step-by-step. Write in your own steps and timeline and check off items as you complete them.

	STEP	HOW LONG TO START BEFORE MOVE	DURATION
EMPLOYMENT			
	Prepare for job search		
☐			
☐			
☐			
☐			
☐			
	Find jobs		
☐			
☐			
☐			
☐			
☐			
☐			
	Accept a job		
☐			
☐			
☐			
☐			
☐			

	STEP	HOW LONG TO START BEFORE MOVE	DURATION
NEW HOME			
	Prepare for home search		
☐			
☐			
☐			
☐			
☐			
☐			
☐			
	Find homes		
☐			
☐			
☐			
☐			
☐			
☐			
☐			
	The transaction		
☐			
☐			
☐			
☐			
☐			

	STEP	HOW LONG TO START BEFORE MOVE	DURATION
PLANNING HOW YOU'LL MOVE			
	Possessions		
☐			
☐			
☐			
☐			
☐			
☐			
☐			
	People		
☐			
☐			
☐			
☐			
☐			
☐			
SAYING GOODBYE			
☐			
☐			
☐			
☐			
☐			
☐			

	STEP	HOW LONG TO START BEFORE MOVE	DURATION
THE MOVE			
	Prepare		
☐			
☐			
☐			
☐			
☐			
☐			
☐			
☐			
☐			
	Pack		
☐			
☐			
☐			
☐			
☐			
☐			
☐			
☐			
☐			
☐			
MOVING DAY			

	STEP	HOW LONG TO START BEFORE MOVE	DURATION
ARRIVE AND MOVE IN			
	When you arrive		
☐			
☐			
☐			
☐			
☐			
	Move In		
☐			
☐			
☐			
☐			
☐			

Once you have your plan filled out, revisit it weekly and update it as you progress. Keep track of any warning signs. For example, if it has been two months and you haven't even finished preparing your résumé, ask yourself how serious you are about relocating. While it's okay to not be in a hurry, this plan will help you be aware of all the separate tasks that do need to be addressed in order to make a successful move.

Setting a Budget

You don't want to run out of gas money sixty miles from your new town, so make sure you set enough money aside. There are the obvious costs to be aware of, like the cost of moving yourself and your things, but there are myriad other expenses to expect, including costs for setting up new utilities, travel before or after your move, and even new clothes for job interviews.

Moving can be expensive. Depending on where and when you're moving, reasonable costs can range from "no expenses" to over $100,000. Here are the biggest factors that affect what you'll pay:

- How much stuff you have

- How you will move it

- When you will move it

- How far you will move it

- How you will move yourself

- Whether you will have to pay sales commissions in buying or selling a home

Once those factors are set, there aren't many other ways to cut costs significantly.

Each chapter of this section includes a low, medium, and high "estimated cost" to give you a ballpark idea of expenses. Your costs are likely to vary from what's in this book. Use the estimated costs as a guide to help you budget, but adjust them to reflect your own circumstances, and populate the Worksheet: Your Budget to create a more accurate budget for yourself.

Example Expense Ranges for Budgeting

EXPENSE	LOW ESTIMATE (DOLLARS)	MEDIUM ESTIMATE (DOLLARS)	HIGH ESTIMATE (DOLLARS)
EMPLOYMENT			
Prepare for job search	0	600	12,000
Find jobs	5	105	1,400
Accept a job	330	1,050	6,100
NEW HOME			
Total cost for renting (including deposit)	1,285	3,210	13,140
Total cost for buying (including down payment and fees)	10,185	40,710	140,340
PLANNING THE MOVE			
Costs for moving yourself and your things	450	4,500	12,500
SAYING GOODBYE			
Costs for closing out your old home	1,590	17,740	55,300
ARRIVE AND MOVE IN			
Costs to move in and settle in	385	1,550	10,400
EXAMPLE TOTAL MOVE COST			
RENTING	**4,010**	**28,710**	**110,790**
BUYING	**12,910**	**66,210**	**237,990**

WORKSHEET: YOUR BUDGET

Use this template to budget for your expenses throughout the moving process. There is a "contingency" line item—basically a fudge factor—recognizing that you can't anticipate everything and it won't all go smoothly, so expect a little more expense than you can predict. At the same time, track your actual costs to see whether you're staying within your budget and can still afford the remaining steps of your relocation.

EXPENSE	ESTIMATED COST	ACTUAL COST
EMPLOYMENT		
NEW HOME		

Expense	Estimated Cost	Actual Cost
Planning The Move		
Saying Goodbye		

Expense	Estimated Cost	Actual Cost
Arrive and Move In		
Subtotal		
Contingency factor (add 10% of subtotal)		
Total		

Once you have a cost estimate, compare that to the amount of money you have available—or will have available if you remain continuously employed during your move. If you can't afford to move now, calculate how much you need to save before you can start working on relocating in earnest.

Start setting money aside or make sure you have enough in savings. Even after the move, there may be unexpected purchases needed for your new home.

If you're being moved by your employer, they might cover many of these expenses for you. Be sure to find out what they will be paying for. If you're moving to an area with a higher cost of living, you could request a corresponding raise.

If yours is a two-career household, agree on whether both of you will be able to remain employed continuously or if there will be a gap in income as one of you seeks a job after moving.

As you spend money, save your receipts so that you can claim a deduction on your taxes (there's more about this in Chapter 14). Write down the actual costs in the Worksheet: Your Budget. If your actual costs are way over your plan, you may need a slightly longer "runway" before you move. If your costs are under budget, then you can start thinking of ways to spend the extra money! Landing a job in your new area could be key to making sure you have enough money.

• • •

A solid plan guides your relocation. It's just a matter of the time it takes to go through each of the steps.

7 Find a Job

If you're just starting college, self-employed, in possession of enough savings, or retired, you may be able to skip this step. However, for many people it's risky to move somewhere without already having lined up a job in their destination city. Being assertive about your job search at the beginning of your planning process will help you gain control of what can be one of the most unpredictable factors in your move.

Let's discuss the steps you can take toward a successful job search, from exploring options to negotiating offers and transitioning to your new job or school.

PLANNING TO FIND A JOB

For people who are "working for the man," it can take some time to find a new job. The time it takes to find a job will vary based on the type of position you are seeking, the demand for your skills in your new city, the overall state of the economy, and other factors—including sheer luck.

MY EXPERIENCE

Before my wife and I moved, we knew that one of us needed to get a job first. So, we set aside one evening per week for both of us to focus on finding a job. We tried looking for jobs from several different angles. We reached out to old contacts, searched for companies in our industries, applied to job boards, and more. By establishing this habit, we knew that our move would happen because we were going to keep looking until we found something.

Step-by-Step Plan

To keep your efforts in perspective, here is a sample plan that reflects the contents of this chapter with suggested timing. You can't necessarily control when you will accept a job, but your timing in going through each step in your plan will affect how soon you'll be able to arrive at your new home. You might want to plan your first steps for finding a home (outlined in the next chapter) to coincide with your visit for job interviews. Use the Worksheet: Your Plan in the previous chapter to fill in your own steps.

	STEP	HOW LONG TO START BEFORE MOVE	DURATION
EMPLOYMENT			
	Prepare for job search	**12–52 weeks**	**1–4 weeks**
1.	Create a plan		
2.	Prepare your résumé		
3.	Build skills and experience		
	Find jobs	**12–52 weeks**	**4–52 weeks**
4.	Search for jobs, employers, and connections		
5.	Submit applications or résumés		

	STEP	HOW LONG TO START BEFORE MOVE	DURATION
	Accept a job	**2–8 weeks**	**2–12 weeks**
6.	Interview		
7.	Choose		
8.	Negotiate and accept		

Budgeting

Your plan should include a budget so that you know what you're prepared to spend and can afford it. While your mileage will vary, there is a low, medium, and high budget estimate included so that you can see how much costs vary and get a sense of where you may be. See the next table for the details behind these estimates and use the Worksheet: Your Budget to create your budget.

Low budget estimate: $335

If you're fortunate, you could get a job without spending any money, such as if you transfer offices or land a job without traveling for an interview. However, odds are you'll have to spend some money to secure a job. If your destination city is a few hours' drive away, you could possibly do a few interviews in a day or two and keep your job-search budget low.

Mid budget estimate: $1,755

An "average" experience might include professional résumé help, a new outfit for interviewing, and traveling at your own expense to an in-person interview in your destination city. Costs will depend on how expensive it is to travel to your destination city and whether your partner or family will accompany you.

High budget estimate: $19,500

Reasons you might incur higher costs might involve seeking an executive position, needing help from service providers like career consultants, taking your family with you, or having multiple rounds of interviews. While a difficult job search can be hard to predict, multiple visits for interviews will escalate your costs.

Example Expenses

EXPENSE	LOW ESTIMATE (DOLLARS)	MEDIUM ESTIMATE (DOLLARS)	HIGH ESTIMATE (DOLLARS)
PREPARE FOR JOB SEARCH			
Career counseling services	0	200	6,000
Résumé preparation	0	250	1,000
Additional education	0	150	5,000
FIND JOBS			
Printing and mailing costs of applications	5	25	200
Additional marketing fees (e.g., LinkedIn, advertisements)	0	30	200
Networking events	0	50	1,000
ACCEPT A JOB			
New attire	0	50	1,000
Transportation expenses (e.g., plane ticket or gasoline)	150	500	2,000
Hotel nights for Interview	100	200	1,500
Local transportation (e.g., rental car, taxi, or public transportation)	40	100	600
Meals during interview travel	40	200	1,000
TOTAL	**335**	**1,755**	**19,500**

PREPARING FOR YOUR JOB SEARCH

It's a good idea to do some mental preparation before you start shotgunning résumés to every company in Columbus. Target the appropriate types of jobs in your search and be prepared to respond quickly if you're contacted for an interview. Be careful not to overdo it and save yourself from job search burnout.

Knowing What You Want

Think about what types of jobs you'd be willing to take.

Freelancers may have the privilege of working from anywhere. People who are looking to establish their own practice of law or medicine may need to make contacts and evaluate the marketplace before moving to an area.

For some people, moving and then finding a temporary or part-time job may be good enough. More flexibility lowers the risk of not getting a job. If you're willing to accept pretty much anything, then you might not need to secure employment before you arrive—assuming you can survive without an income at least until you land that first job.

On the other hand, taking just any job could be a step backward, making it harder to eventually find employment in your field and income bracket. Depending on your circumstances, landing a job before moving is usually the best plan—even if it delays your relocation.

Review your experience, reflect on your strengths, and look through different types of jobs; widen your awareness of all of your options and potential interests. You can identify what field interests you, what type of employer you could see yourself working for, or a couple of different job titles that could fit you well.

Be aware that searching for a job at a distance makes something that's already difficult (finding a job) even harder. Decide whether to add any more levels of difficulty—for example, by aiming for a promotion or even changing careers.

Build Skills and Experience

The positions you are interested in may require skills or certifications beyond those you currently have. There may be specific state licensing requirements for your profession if you're an engineer or a teacher, for example. Or the kinds of projects in your new city could have a different industry focus than what you're used to. Issues for someone in your position might be much different, such as in public service or natural resources jobs. Identify the gaps between your experience and the requirements of the types of jobs you want. The earlier in the process that you recognize these weaknesses, the easier it will be to bridge the gaps.

Focus on growing your existing skills and catering them to the types of jobs you're finding in your target city. You may consider volunteering, continuing classroom education, taking on new assignments at work, or pursuing a professional license. You might even look into attending industry conferences or workshops in your new area, both to network and to learn about what's relevant in that region. If you work in a creative field, build your portfolio as much as possible.

Challenges from a Distance

Applying for a job far away from you puts you at a slight disadvantage as many employers prefer dealing with local candidates.

If you sense a hesitancy to hire out-of-state candidates, you might improve your chances of being contacted by listing a phone number local to your employer. You could accomplish this by purchasing a new mobile phone plan or using Google Voice. Some people choose to hide their address from their résumés, though this can raise suspicion.

If you are called for an interview, you will likely be asked why you're interested in relocating near their office. You may want to convey your seriousness by explaining that you're expecting to move there within the next few months.

Employers could be concerned that you may be relocating on a whim and won't stay in the area long. If you indicate that you plan to stay for at least two years, or have family connections in the area, hiring managers will see you as a more stable option.

Many employers are not willing to pay relocation costs, so if you are not expecting a relocation package, you could indicate that. Also, your willingness to participate fully in the interview process, including traveling for an interview, should help your candidacy. It certainly can't harm it.

My Experience

When we were ready to get serious about our job search, we began by preparing our résumés and publishing them online so that they were searchable on the big job sites and some of the smaller sites as well.

Since I was interested in positions in two different fields in which I had experience, I prepared two unique résumés and cover letters that I could use accordingly for each particular job I applied to.

In my cover letters, I said that I would be available to work in Seattle in February so that hiring managers knew my timing for relocating. When companies asked why we were moving, we just explained that we were planning a move and wanted a change without a lot of specifics. That seemed to work fine.

FINDING YOUR DREAM JOB

There are a number of different ways to find specific jobs to apply for. A 2014 study by CareerXroads found that 19% of recent hires got their job through networking, another 19% through a company website, and 15% through online job boards (Crispin 2014). Other sources have networking as an even more common way of landing a job.

With the variety of methods that could be effective, you probably want to try a few of them.

Once you've started applying to jobs, keep a record of the companies you've contacted and positions that you've applied for. This makes it easier for you to follow up with a letter or phone call a couple of weeks later.

Talking to Others

For some people, "networking" has a bad connotation, but letting friends and acquaintances know you're trying to find a new job can work in your favor. Look for ways to help others with their careers and they will return the favor.

Seek out Informational Interviews

Reach out to a company you're interested in, someone you've worked for in the past, or a person you know in your new place, and ask for an informational interview during a visit to your new city or by phone. During informational interviews, ask people what they like about their jobs, what advice they'd give to someone in their industry, how they'd describe the job market and work culture in your prospective area, and whether they can give you contact information for anyone who is hiring or anyone else you should talk to.

Informational interviews can lead to job offers, but that's not their real purpose. They are for gathering information and making contacts along your career trajectory and can be a useful tool in the long-distance job search. Informational interviews work best if you can find a way to eventually reciprocate in some way to benefit the people you meet with.

Applying Directly

Find Companies That Appeal

Identify some key employers that you may be interested in working for. You may already know of large companies located at your destination. Investigate further to explore smaller companies there. Ask your existing contacts—including those you've made through informational interviews—to suggest any potential employers in your field of interest. The Internet can also be a good tool for finding "advertising firms in Albuquerque," "construction companies in Colorado Springs," and everything in between. You can find lists of employers in certain fields through professional associations, regulatory bodies, or searches on online directories such as the Yellow Pages.

Once you've identified some companies of interest, visit their websites to search for job openings. Even if your ideal job isn't posted, a cover letter and résumé that you submit for a related job can make it to the right person that needs someone with your specific skills.

Maybe you'd prefer to distinguish yourself with a more personal touch. Try mailing a letter, making a cold call, finding a contact through LinkedIn, or even stopping by the office. Smaller companies receive fewer applications out of the blue than do the larger ones, so you might be more likely to get a callback if you apply to them. Just remember not to come on too strong; research each target company and choose a strategy that seems to fit their specific culture and values.

Review Job Boards

Many websites are out there, including niche job sites, regional job boards, and major job search websites, that let you search for jobs and post your résumé. Most of these sites allow you to hide your name in case you don't want your current employer to find out.

There are many jobs available on various job boards that offer filtering and alert features to help you find the types of positions you are seeking. The Online Resources section at the end of this book lists job websites, including options for international searches.

Attend Job Fairs

If you're in town looking for a job, a job fair introduces you to companies that are hiring. Often a local newspaper or job board service will sponsor a public job fair. Local colleges often host job fairs with employers who are primarily looking to hire college graduates, but you may be able to enter the job fair for a fee.

> ### My Experience
>
> *We started our active job search by looking at job postings online. For the first few weeks, it was very time consuming to filter the search results enough that they would turn up some positions that we were interested in and qualified for. It took patience and persistence, but after a few weeks, we became adept at finding the occupations that looked like a good fit for us by quickly looking for specific keywords, locations, and employers.*
>
> *In addition to searching online job boards, we also identified companies of interest in our prospective cities. We looked at the major companies that employ people in our fields. We also looked for smaller local employers that we could apply to.*
>
> *After several weeks spent reviewing job postings and submitting our résumés unsolicited, we became frustrated by the lack of interviews. Neither of us had any promising contact with employers.*
>
> *We wondered whether we should just move and search for a job later, but in the end we stuck to our original plan. We resolved not to settle or give in; rather than panic or get frustrated, we knew we should trust the sheer power of persistence.*

Other Options

Look into Transfers and Telecommuting

If you're employed by an organization that has other locations, perhaps you can put in a request to relocate. Some companies have restrictions on transferring or very limited positions in your destination city. Other companies might have job openings that you could apply for, or allow you more flexibility in job duties—or even allow telecommuting.

If your company lets you work remotely, you could make your own workspace wherever you live. Depending on your situation and workspace preferences, it may be well worth inquiring about. Be careful about when and how you ask; you don't want to put the company on notice that you might leave before you're ready to tell them.

Investigate Staffing Agencies and Other Services

Staffing agencies work on the employers' behalf and at their expense to fill open job postings. They can connect you to employers who are hiring and can be another resource on the local hiring climate.

Search for staffing agencies regional to your new area or focused on your industry. While some staffing agencies focus on temporary or contract work, many place full-time employees as well.

If you have additional job search questions or challenges, you might look for other resources. There are other service providers who will edit your résumé and consult with you throughout your job search. These often cost money but can be great if you need some extra help. Look for additional job search advice online and in books that focus on jobs.

ACCEPTING A JOB

Interviewing

Employers often review résumés with an emphasis on your hard-and-fast qualifications, and then use interviews to gauge your fit for the specific organization and its culture.

> ## MY EXPERIENCE
>
> *We found one successful trick for landing interviews. We planned a trip to Seattle and contacted various people (HR, hiring managers, other contacts) and suggested meeting when we were in town. Since we were taking the trouble to go all the way to Seattle and would only be available for a couple days, we got a pretty positive response from people willing to take advantage of the opportunity to meet with us. Many of those people didn't have a position open immediately, but those meetings helped us understand the employment landscape and build a relationship.*
>
> *My employer didn't know we were applying for jobs. Throughout this process, I didn't tell many people about our plans to move, but I knew I would eventually have to tell my employer that I needed time off to travel to the Northwest. When I asked for that time off, I explained that we would be visiting the Northwest without sharing a lot of details about what the trip was for. I explained that I'd never been to the Northwest and was looking forward to visiting it, although I didn't exactly say that it was a vacation.*
>
> *When companies asked us when we could move there, we picked a date about six weeks after our interviews based on when our apartment lease was ending and how quickly we thought we could move.*

Once you are invited to interview at a company, prepare for your appointment by running through interview practice questions. Spend some time to investigate the company, their business model, their competitors, and current issues in the news that may affect them. Be prepared to discuss these topics and share anecdotes of unique or challenging situations you've handled before. Be ready to problem-solve on the spot should you need to answer any scenario-based interview questions. Also be comfortable talking about yourself, your strengths and weaknesses, and why you want the job.

Try to determine when you think you can move so that companies can set a start date. If you won't be able to move for six months, for instance, companies may be hesitant to wait for you.

After you've traveled all the way to your destination for the interview, *do* make sure to show up early and dress appropriately.

Choosing

You must decide how selective you will be when that first job offer comes in.

Is your compensation package competitive within the local economy? And while salary is an easily measured aspect of a job, other factors—such as the hours you'll be expected to work, the office culture, and the benefits—can have a greater effect on your happiness and in your career path. Does the job take you in the right direction for your career and provide you enough money and free time to enjoy your dream city?

Here are a few scenarios that you could find yourself in:

- An offer might not feel right and could take your career in the wrong direction. This could make you even less marketable than you were before accepting the job.

- If you find the company's benefits stingy or their dress code stifling to your productivity, then it may not matter if the job is otherwise the perfect fit. You might want to remove yourself from the process if you realize that the job isn't a good fit for you.

- Perhaps the position itself isn't the best fit, but you really like the company or the industry and can aim to change positions in the months or years after you get on board.

- If the job offer is a "mixed bag" but has a lot of potential, look into negotiating a higher salary, a moving allowance, or more vacation time.

- You might be offered an exciting position at a great place to work— that should make your decision easy!

Make sure you get your job offer in writing. The offer should be very specific and include a salary and start date.

> My Experience
>
> *I have a friend who moved out of state to take video on an exotic animal farm. He loaded his car with everything he needed to live there for a few months and showed up one afternoon. When he got there, the producer was surprised and the job offer that had seemed so certain turned out not to be final. Fortunately, it was only a three-hour drive, but still a hard lesson to learn.*

As you mull over all these points, you may want to discuss your offer with close family, but not with coworkers until everything is lined up. If you have difficulty deciding whether to accept, you can try one of the decision-making techniques suggested in Chapter 5. You may not find the perfect position at a great company in your ideal industry that pays well, but if you receive an acceptable offer, saying "yes" will set your relocation in motion.

> My Experience
>
> *Our visit for interviews was successful and Lesley was offered a job—her top choice of all the places she interviewed at. Once that happened, we knew we were on our way to Seattle.*

Accepting the New and Quitting the Old

Once you decide whether to accept a job, write an acceptance or rejection letter to the employer. Regardless of your response, express your appreciation for the job offer. If you're rejecting it, do it tactfully, as sometime in the future you might want another chance to work for the same company or for the same hiring manager.

Before telling your current employer that you're leaving, learn what their procedures are for departing employees. Some bosses won't let you take days off after giving notice, so consider taking some final days off to run errands or have movers estimate the weight of your belongings.

Don't forget details like health insurance. If your coverage ends on your last day of work, take your family in for checkups *before* that date and buy private insurance to cover you between jobs if necessary.

Once you do put in your notice at your current employer, be prepared for a wide range of reactions. Some companies won't want you to serve out your two weeks; in fact, they might even send you home and pack up your desk for you. Or, your current employer could give you a counter-offer with a nice raise.

In your final working days, you might feel guilty about leaving or even feel shunned, but you'll have plenty of other things to do in the lead-up to your move.

Spend your last two weeks wisely and productively. You can spend lunch or after-work time picking up moving supplies or dropping off donated items and returning borrowed items to coworkers. Focus on making the most of these days before your departure and bringing good closure to this chapter of your life. Don't burn any bridges, even if you don't anticipate ever coming back. You never know when you will need to call on someone you previously worked with for a favor or a reference.

AFTER LANDING A JOB

Once you've accepted a new job, one of the biggest risks of your relocation plan will be out of the way. You'll be able to shift gears toward the details of your move.

You may want to keep your new employer posted about your progress as you look for housing and plan a moving date. If you find you need more time, let your new employer know as soon as possible.

Anticipate other scenarios; if your new position is unionized, you may need to join the union before you can start work.

If yours is a double-income family and only one of you has found a job so far, you'll need to make more specific arrangements. The one who hasn't landed a new job yet may need to be out of work for a little while. If you can temporarily afford to be on a single income after relocating, the jobless one of you can coordinate most of the move-in while the employed one works.

My Experience

After Lesley received a job offer, I let my boss know that we'd be moving. Since I hadn't received a job offer in Seattle yet, I expressed an interest in working from home in Seattle to ease the transition for my boss and for me. He agreed. I worked from home for the first six months in Seattle, and the company flew me back to Texas for company business several times. That couldn't go on forever, as they hired my replacement about the same time that I found my next job.

• • •

Now that you have a job, moving is no longer a goal but an actual event that will happen. Any uncertainty about being able to move should melt away, making the rest of the steps to your new home easier, though there's still a lot of work to do.

8 Find a New Home

Once you've determined which city to live in and know what work you'll be doing there, it's time to find a home.

Think about starting this process before securing a job; once you've already lined up employment and have a start date, you might not have much time left to find a neighborhood and housing.

Let's walk through the process: from determining what type of place you want to live in, evaluating different areas and dwellings, narrowing down your options, to completing the transaction by either buying or renting.

ORGANIZING YOUR HOME SEARCH

When choosing a home, you'll want to determine the areas of town you'd be willing to live in, and then find a place that fits your budget and other criteria.

Circumstances may well dictate whether you apply for a new home sight unseen or spend a few days in town having a realtor show you around.

Cathy Goodwin, career planner and author of the book, *Making the Big Move: How to Transform Relocation into a Creative Life Transition*, says that people spend more time selecting a car than a home.

Don't make that mistake; choosing the right home in the right neighborhood is key to having a good experience in your new city.

Determining Your Living Arrangement

What type of arrangement do you want in your new home? Will you be staying with family? Are you buying a house? Here are some possibilities to evaluate:

- **Short-term rental:** If you have little time to invest now in finding a permanent home, select a furnished rental or extended stay apartment where you can live for your first few weeks in town. Once you're in town, it's easier to search for the right area and a long-term home.

- **Looking for a roommate:** If you're moving on your own, you could consider finding a roommate who can introduce you to the city or at least share the rent. Moving in with someone you haven't met before is common in big cities and can be a good way to save money.

- **Staying with someone you know:** Crashing on someone's couch can be inexpensive and put you in contact with people who know the area until you get a job or find your own place. This option might not last long if your personalities clash, but it can be a good way for a single person to start off in a new city.

- **Cohousing:** This is another cost-effective option that gets you a private room with some shared amenities such as a kitchen and garden. People usually choose cohousing for its intentional community environment.

- **Rent a home on your own:** Available rental options include suburban apartment complexes, urban apartment buildings, single homes, duplexes, townhomes, and other arrangements. Even if you want to buy a residence, renting can be a good short-term option until you find the right home for you. By renting, you will have fewer maintenance responsibilities and can move once your lease ends. Some rentals provide events where you can meet your neighbors.

- **Buy a condominium:** Condos, townhomes, or other alternatives to the traditional single-family home can be less expensive than buying a house, though they have homeowners' association dues or common fees that can add up. The homeowners' association will enforce rules or restrictions that apply to everyone involved. Buying a condo provides some of the advantages of homeownership, like accruing equity, but with fewer maintenance responsibilities.

- **Buy a house:** If you already know which area you want to live in or don't want to have to move again anytime soon, buying a home can be a wise long-term financial investment and provide an opportunity to have pride in ownership. Look into whether you want to buy a brand-new home or an older one. Building your own home presents a whole separate set of challenges that are doubled if you will be coordinating the construction from a distance.

Renting Versus Buying

Deciding whether to rent or own can be a complicated decision. Renting can keep your life simpler and more flexible, but buying will help you to build equity and give you roots in an area.

If you're contemplating whether to buy or rent, think through these factors:

- **Attitude and plans:** If buying, you should probably foresee staying put for at least five years. Think about your future and whether you'll be raising a family—will you have enough space? Will you have kids and struggle to pay for their college while still paying your mortgage?

- **Local knowledge:** It can take some time before you understand the nuances of which parts of town fit you and your lifestyle best. Would you rather rent for a while to gain local knowledge, or do you feel comfortable with how much you know about an area that you could purchase a home before moving there?

- **Available time and money to invest in maintenance:** Are you okay with spending time regularly to repair leaky pipes and unclogging sinks (or paying someone to fix them for you), or would you rather call the landlord or property management company to take care of things?

- **Your assets:** Can you afford to make a down payment on a home? If moving expenses will eat a big chunk of your savings, you might not be in the best position to immediately make a down payment on a new home and pay for closing costs, taxes, and other expenditures that come with a home purchase.

- **Your income:** Monthly payments for buying and renting can be comparable, but some housing markets are different. Experts advise keeping rent or mortgage costs below one-quarter of your income or one-third of your income at most. Your credit score and market factors will affect the terms for your mortgage, which can influence whether buying is a good option for you.

- **Income stability:** If you are just starting a new job, it could be risky to invest in owning a home, especially if you have multiple people to support with one income. The new job might not work out or there could be instability at the company that you weren't aware of. Perhaps you have other income sources, or you and your partner both have fairly secure jobs that make a commitment to mortgage payments less risky.

- **The market:** Are home prices low or high? Rent prices tend to be more stable than buying prices. If housing prices dip when you try to sell, you could be in a tough spot. Beware of buying in an area of declining values as it may be harder to resell.

- **Financing conditions:** Your monthly payment will vary based on your credit score, but if interest rates are low, your monthly mortgage payment will be more affordable.

Creating a Plan to Find a Home

Which is more important to you: the neighborhood in which you live or the actual dwelling? This answer will influence how you approach your home search.

You might prefer to find your perfect neighborhood before zeroing in on a home, or you'd rather start looking for advertised homes and then factor the neighborhoods into your evaluation.

In reality, neighborhoods and types of homes are related. You might want to live in a hip urban center, but if you also want a large, newly-built, ranch-style home, there may not be any options available.

Consider how many trips you're willing to take prior to your move to visit places. Can you squeeze in time to look at neighborhoods and residences during job interview visits?

Here is a sample plan you can use to outline your home search and update the Worksheet: Your Plan in Chapter 6.

Step-by-Step Plan

	STEP	HOW LONG TO START BEFORE MOVE	DURATION
NEW HOME			
	Prepare for home search	**12–26 weeks**	**1–4 weeks**
1.	Create a plan		
2.	Establish your criteria		
	Find homes	**8–20 weeks**	**4–39 weeks**
3.	Find and explore neighborhoods		
4.	Visit homes		
5.	Make a decision		
	The transaction	**2–8 weeks**	**1–6 weeks**
6.	Apply or submit your offer		
7.	Sign on the dotted line		

Budgeting

Travel costs to visit your new area to tour homes can significantly affect your costs, and up-front costs for buying will be much higher than costs for renting. A common down payment is 20% of the sale price and closing costs around 6% are typical.

Low budget rental estimate: $1,285
If you're moving to an inexpensive rental and don't have to pay for a pet deposit, your up-front home costs could be fairly low.

Mid budget rental estimate: $3,210
Most rentals will require various deposits and up-front fees.

High budget rental estimate: $13,140
More time spent traveling to look for higher-end places will affect your costs.

Low budget purchase estimate: $10,185
A starter home in an inexpensive area can keep your up-front costs low.

Mid budget purchase estimate: $40,710
A higher down payment will require you to have more cash but will decrease the interest paid over the life of the loan.

High budget purchase estimate: $140,340
You can pay as much of a down payment as you can afford, as long as you leave some money for expenses in the first few months after relocating.

Example Expenses

EXPENSE	LOW ESTIMATE (DOLLARS)	MEDIUM ESTIMATE (DOLLARS)	HIGH ESTIMATE (DOLLARS)
FIND HOMES			
Transportation expenses (e.g., plane ticket or gasoline)	50	200	2,000
Hotel nights to look for place	50	200	1,500
Local transportation (e.g., rental car, taxi, or public transportation)	40	100	600
Food during travel	40	200	1,200
TRANSACTION			
Mailing signed documents	5	10	40
RENTING			
Security deposit—often one to two months' rent	500	1,200	5,000
Pet deposit	100	200	300
First month's rent	500	1,100	2,500
BUYING			
Home Closing Costs This can vary depending on how much the seller pays.	5,000	15,000	35,000
Down Payment The larger the down payment, the less you'll have to pay on a monthly basis, and the less interest you will pay over the lifetime of the loan.	5,000	25,000	100,000
TOTAL FOR RENTING	1,285	3,210	13,140
TOTAL FOR BUYING	10,185	40,710	140,340

ESTABLISHING YOUR CRITERIA

What Matters in a Neighborhood?

Whether renting or buying, limit your search to specific areas that you would want to live in. As with choosing a city, the locale you choose in that city will depend on what's important to you.

The criteria you identified in Chapter 3 are probably still important in choosing a neighborhood, though some criteria won't apply.

If you decide to move to Tucson for sun and warmth, any area of Tucson will have the weather you're looking for. However, other criteria will matter. If you're moving to Florida for the beaches, look for places to live that are within a mile of the beach. Sometimes the importance of other criteria will have changed: finding a safe city might not have been a top priority, but locating a safe neighborhood in it might be.

Choose the right area for your situation. If you have children, make sure the schools are acceptable and the kids will have places to play. If you're single, you may prefer to live in an area that offers more opportunities to hang out with people your age.

You probably want to choose a location based on how you spend your time. If you shop often, consider living near a mall or shopping district. If you like to walk, look for housing near parks or in a walkable urban area. If you anticipate many medical appointments, look for somewhere to live in or near the medical district. If you'll be commuting regularly, you may want to live near work to save time at the beginning and end of your day. If you have any special needs, such as a medical condition, look for guidance on finding a good location near the support you'd like to have.

Refer back to Chapter 4 for sources of information you can reference in your search. You could buy a city map or use an online map to aid your search. Pinpoint key attractions, such as your employer, schools, grocery stores, parks, public transit lines, or anything else that's important to you. As you research neighborhoods, highlight areas that seem to meet your needs.

Use the Worksheet: Evaluating a Neighborhood to help you assess different parts of town that you've identified.

WORKSHEET: EVALUATING A NEIGHBORHOOD

Fill out this worksheet for each neighborhood you consider. Make copies of the blank worksheet in this book or download the worksheet from www.ARelocationHandbook.com. The criteria in this worksheet are grouped by "Proximity" and "Area."

1. Fill out the *Weight* column to indicate the importance of each aspect of a neighborhood. These values will be the same for each neighborhood you evaluate:

    For "must-haves," assign a weight of 10

    For "should-haves," assign a weight of 4

    For "nice-to-haves," assign a weight of 1

    If not relevant, assign a weight of 0

2. Fill out a numerical *Rating* for each aspect of the neighborhood you're evaluating:

    exceeds expectations = 2

    meets expectations = 1

    acceptable = 0

    unsatisfactory = -1

3. Calculate a *Score* for each row by multiplying the *Weight* value by the *Rating* value.

4. Add up the *Score* values for each section and write-in the total value at the bottom of each part of the worksheet.

5. As you complete this worksheet for different areas, hone in on neighborhoods with the highest total scores.

Neighborhood: _____

PROXIMITY: HOW CONVENIENTLY LOCATED IS THIS TO OTHER PLACES IN YOUR DAILY LIFE?			
TOPIC	WEIGHT	RATING	SCORE
Transportation: How easy is it to get around from here? Look at things like walkability, sidewalk infrastructure, bike paths, transit service, traffic levels, availability of street parking, and convenience to the freeway.			
Workplace: How far away would you be from work? Do you want a 30-minute commute to help clear your head after work, or would you like to be so close that you can walk home for lunch? (Look into the commute; a ten-minute drive on Sunday afternoon could take several times as long during rush hour.)			
Schools: How close is your university or how good are the schools where your children would go? School district boundaries can seem arbitrary, so make sure you know where the border is. Even if you don't have children, the quality of a school district can affect the resale value of your home.			
Grocery store: Is there a store nearby for regular shopping or a corner store for pantry staples?			
Services: Can you perform errands easily, like going to the bank, dropping off a library book, or getting your nails done?			
Communications: Are you within reliable cell phone coverage? Do the networks that are important to you (e.g., DSL, cable, or fiber) reach the area?			
Health care: Are there doctor's offices, medical clinics, or hospitals nearby? Could you get to a hospital quickly in case of an emergency?			

Topic	Weight	Rating	Score
Restaurants: Are there restaurants around that serve the types of food you like in the price range you're looking for?			
Coffee shops: Is there a place nearby to grab your morning latte or where you can spend an afternoon on your laptop?			
Bars: Are there places where you would feel comfortable going for a drink after work or meeting up with friends?			
Parks and recreation: Look for neighborhood parks you can stroll through and playgrounds for your little one. Is there a community center or beach nearby?			
Entertainment: How far are you from a movie theater, performing arts center, or sports arena?			
Shopping: Do you make frequent trips to home improvement stores or the mall?			
Other: List other things you'd like to be conveniently located to:			
Other:			
Other:			
Proximity Total Score			

Area: How desirable is the neighborhood?			
Topic	Weight	Rating	Score
Safety: Would you be comfortable walking this neighborhood at night? Will metal bars be needed on your windows? Are the roadways particularly dangerous? Look up "Meghan's Law" to see if any sex offenders live here.			
Character and aesthetics: Is it important to you to have local establishments, old homes, historical architecture, or mature trees nearby? What is unique about the neighborhood? Are homes and yards well maintained?			
Neighborhood demographics: Who lives here? Are neighbors retired or families with teenage children? Could you be comfortable living with the people in the area?			
Affordability: Are these homes within your price range? Even if the average price is too high for you, could you possibly find a smaller home or fixer-upper that would work?			
Area trajectory: Your neighborhood will change over time. Is this area on an upswing or downward trend? Try to learn the city's plans for the area. How is it zoned? Are there buildings under construction? Will road widening or new highway construction slice through the neighborhood or create more traffic?			
Other: List other things that are important characteristics of your neighborhood:			
Other:			
Other:			
Neighborhood Total Score			

What Matters in a Home?

Envision what your home looks like. Is it a large house on a quiet street? Does it offer a view of the city? Would you rather have a new modern home or an older one with charm and character?

Just as your neighborhood will reflect your lifestyle, the specific type of place you live in will as well. Determine what's important to you in a home as nowhere will be perfect. You will likely have to compromise on some things. Differentiate between what would be *nice* to have, and what you really think you need.

> MY EXPERIENCE
>
> *This is one area where my wife and I weren't completely on the same page. I wanted to save money and would have been content with an older and less up-to-date apartment unit. However, it was important to Lesley that our home have modern amenities and be in good condition. In the end, I realized that we couldn't make a bad decision. I was happy to choose her preferred place, so that we could have an even nicer place to live (and she would be happy).*

You can use the Worksheet: Evaluating a Home to identify the importance of each aspect.

WORKSHEET: EVALUATING A HOME

Fill out this worksheet for each home you're interested in. Make copies of the blank worksheet in this book or download the worksheet from www.ARelocationHandbook.com. The worksheet is divided into sections of "Basic Needs," "Comfort and Lifestyle," "Home Unit," and "Systems."

1. Fill out the *Weight* column to indicate the importance of each aspect of a house. If you're planning to buy, share the worksheet with your realtor to help him or her find the right place for you. These values will be the same for each home you evaluate.

    For "must-haves," assign a weight of 10

    For "should-haves," assign a weight of 4

    For "nice-to-haves," assign a weight of 1

    If not relevant, assign a weight of 0

2. Fill out a numerical *Rating* for each aspect of the neighborhood you're evaluating:

    exceeds expectations = 2

    meets expectations = 1

    acceptable = 0

    unsatisfactory = -1

3. Calculate a *Score* for each row by multiplying the *Weight* value by the *Rating* value.

4. Add up the *Score* values for each section and write-in the total value at the bottom of each part of the worksheet.

5. Choose a home with high total scores.

Address: _____

Home Description: _____

Date Visited: _____

BASIC NEEDS: HOW WELL DOES THE HOME MEET YOUR FUNDAMENTAL NEEDS?			
TOPIC	WEIGHT	RATING	SCORE
Base cost: What will you have to pay either to purchase the place or for your monthly rent payment?			
Repair and maintenance cost: Does this place require significant repairs? If you buy it, do you expect there to be high ongoing maintenance costs?			
What's included: A high cost can be a good value if utilities, appliances, or furniture are included. Are there parking fees or a neighborhood association you're required to join?			
Safety: Is the place itself safe? Look for deadbolt locks on all the external doors. Is exterior lighting adequate? Does the building adhere to current fire codes and seismic standards? If renting, is there a sprinkler system in the building? Is safe parking included?			
Lease term: Do you want to stay for a year, or would you rather have the flexibility to leave after six months?			
Other: List other things you'd consider basic needs:			
Other:			
Other:			
BASIC NEEDS TOTAL SCORE			

Comfort and Lifestyle: How suitable is this home for the way you live?			
Topic	Weight	Rating	Score
Yard, outdoors, and view: Consider what you see out of the kitchen window: nature, a city skyline, a street, a brick wall, or a nice big yard? Is there a place to garden? Are trees in good health? Will grass be easy to mow? Is there a deck or balcony? Will you have access to a swimming pool?			
Quiet: Ask neighbors about noise before you commit. Even if this is a quiet area, sit down and listen—what do you hear? Do some neighbors drive loud motorcycles? Are there children? Does your neighbor mow the grass at 6am? Visit at a few different times of day if you can.			
Aesthetically pleasing: Does the place look good? Are the finishes nice? Is the architecture appealing? If in a condo or apartment building, are the public spaces clean?			
Recreation: Does the apartment building have recreation options or a community room? Does the subdivision include a community center?			
Facilities: Is there an area where you can work on your car if you want to? Are there bike lockers? Does this area offer recycling or composting services?			
Pets: Are pets allowed? Are additional fees required?			
Other: List other characteristics and amenities you'd like for your comfort and lifestyle:			
Other:			
Other:			
Comfort and Lifestyle Total Score			

Home Unit: What is the size, shape, condition, and feature set inside the home?			
Topic	Weight	Rating	Score
Size: Is the place the right size? Will your furniture fit? Check available storage: closets, attic space, a shed, or extra garage space. Are the common areas large enough if you want to entertain? Are there enough bathrooms?			
Floor plan: How do you like the layout? If you'll be sharing with a roommate, are the bedrooms separate enough from common areas?			
Condition: Is the building in good shape? Do doors and windows fit snugly into their frames? Are there signs of mortar work or cracks in the walls? Are there any water spots on the ceiling or issues with the plumbing or electrical system? If you're buying a resale home, look for a paper trail of receipts, repairs, upgrades, and services over the years. Is the rental maintained well? Does the landlord take good care of things? Will your maintenance requests be addressed promptly?			
Kitchen: Check the condition of appliances. If you prefer a gas or electric stove, is it the type you want? Is there a dishwasher? Are the cabinets and counters at a comfortable height and are there enough of them? Are there enough electrical outlets for countertop appliances and are they well placed? If you cook a lot, does the layout work for you?			
Bathroom: Is there enough counter space? Is there a bathtub? Check the working condition of faucets, shower heads, flushing mechanisms, drains, and ventilation fans. Does anything need to be replaced?			

Topic	Weight	Rating	Score
Laundry: Is a washer/dryer furnished in this unit? If there's a shared laundry room, ask to see it—is it clean and are the machines working?			
Other: List other characteristics and qualities you'd like to have:			
Other:			
Other:			
Home Unit Total Score			

SYSTEMS: HOW ARE THE SYSTEMS THAT MAKE UP THE HOME?			
TOPIC	WEIGHT	RATING	SCORE
Electrical: Can you run a hair dryer without tripping the circuit breaker? Are there enough electrical outlets? Are the outlets grounded?			
Plumbing: Are there any signs of leaks? Is there strong water pressure? Does the water get hot quickly? Are the sinks and showers what you want? Is there a septic tank and leach field or is the home connected to a municipal sewage system?			
HVAC systems: Does this home have electric, natural gas, or oil heating? What kind of air conditioner, if any, does it have? Do systems seem efficient, safe, and easy to maintain? Are the vents or the heating elements located in a good position to keep you comfortable and not be in the way?			
Lighting: Are rooms well lit? Do any fixtures need replacing?			
Floors: Is there hardwood or carpet flooring? Will the carpet need to be replaced? Is any tile in good condition?			
Modern amenities: Does the unit have a fireplace, energy-efficient windows, or other features not already mentioned?			
Other: List other important criteria for the systems you want:			
Other:			
Other:			
SYSTEMS TOTAL SCORE			

FINDING YOUR DREAM HOME

Once you have an idea of the type of neighborhood and type of home you're looking for, it's time to single out your dream home.

Exploring Neighborhoods

If at all possible, try to physically explore neighborhoods in your destination, either on your first visit, or on a special trip with your family once your job is lined up.

If you can't physically visit, use an online street view or aerial view tool to get a feel for the neighborhoods.

Review the section in Chapter 4 on visiting your destination location for ideas on specific things to look for.

Observe how clean the area is and try to pick up on clues. Are there toys in people's yards? Do people wave at you from their porch? Is there shattered glass on the street?

Notice the non-residential places in the immediate area, such as houses of religion, retail shops, and medical offices.

Try to glean more than just a surface perception. Visit the grocery store, eat at a neighborhood café, and walk around the block. Ask local people their opinions on safety, noise, and anything else you'd like to find out. If you can, spend time in the area at night. Do people stay out late or is it quiet after dark?

Document your findings on the Worksheet: Evaluating a Neighborhood.

As you go through the area, write down names of realtors who have homes advertised or pick up brochures for apartments that you pass by. Pick up a local home or apartment guide to help you find options.

MY EXPERIENCE

We planned to look for places to live during our job interview trip and made a short list of neighborhoods that fit our needs. Then, when we visited, we viewed apartments in those areas with available units. Once Lesley accepted a job offer, we contacted our top apartment choice to request an application and mailed it in.

Finding a Home Online

Whether you are buying or renting, there are numerous resources online to help you find a home.

The Online Resources section at the end of the book lists a number of websites that can be useful for evaluating neighborhoods, searching for rentals, or finding homes for sale.

Getting Help

A rental broker or realtor can be very helpful in orienting you to areas with homes and finding specific options.

Not all real estate agents are realtors; realtors have to agree to a set of ethical guidelines and participate in continuing education courses to be approved by the National Board of Realtors. You can check to see if your realtor belongs to the Multiple Listing Service (MLS) and any local realty groups. Realtors can be separated into buying agents and selling agents.

Of all homes for sale, 85% of them are listed through an agent. If choosing an agent, find a few online and then have a phone conversation first, or meet in person, to find someone who is responsive to your questions by phone, email, or whatever method you prefer. Ask about their experience in finding the type of home you want. Choose someone you feel comfortable with who understands what you're looking for.

There are also apartment hunting services which often work with select properties and are usually paid for by the property manager rather than by the renter. They typically only handle properties that require a background check for all residents, which means that they are more likely to find you a safer home. If you have specific criteria, like wanting a short-term lease, or are having difficulty finding places on your own, these services might be able to find you what you're looking for.

To help your agent serve you, fill out the "importance" column in the Worksheet: Evaluating a Home and Worksheet: Evaluating a Neighborhood, and share these worksheets.

Narrowing Down Options

As you find homes, make a list of them with their websites or phone numbers, and cross off the ones that don't meet your criteria. As you evaluate online and visit in person, use the Worksheet: Evaluating a Home to assess the viable options. If you visit in person, consider taking pictures or using your phone to record your thoughts.

Realize that you might have to compromise a little. If you want that particular view, you might have to accept a place with low water pressure. Or maybe to get such a large home, you'll have to pay to upgrade the kitchen and bathrooms once you move in.

Make sure the options you're considering don't have any special restrictions that would constrain your lifestyle. For example, check with your new city to see if there are any special pet restrictions. The number of pets per household could be limited. Some exotic pets or even some dog breeds that have been deemed dangerous could be banned. If your city allows your pet, make sure that your property manager does too (if you're leasing) or your home ownership group (if it applies).

If you're interested in an apartment building, find out about the *specific units* they have available. The model unit might have great views, but that doesn't mean much if you'll be in a basement unit. Ask to see the particular unit if possible.

If you trust your realtor or apartment agency, they may be willing to take a video of a home or unit you're interested in to help you decide.

Be aware of the local market—if there is strong competition and available housing disappears within days or even hours, you shouldn't spend too much time mulling over your options! The Worksheet: Evaluating a Home can help you determine if a home is a good option. Evaluate at least two homes in an area to give you a better idea of the quality of options there.

MY EXPERIENCE

After our initial move to Seattle, we have moved within Seattle a couple times. On our most recent move, we checked the home listings regularly for several months. By the time we were ready to commit to signing a lease, we were very familiar with the types of homes on the market and the areas where we could live within our price range. It happened that the next home that became available looked like a good value in a good location, so we went ahead and applied without touring any other places.

THE TRANSACTION

For Renting: Applying and Signing the Lease

Even from your old place, you can call a landlord or realtor to request an application to fill out and submit remotely.

It's wise to ask how applications will be processed. Often, it's first come, first served, but you could include a special note or a photo of yourself to try to tip the odds in your favor in a competitive housing market. If you sense that the manager has a number of available units to lease, you might be able to negotiate for upgraded appliances or a new paint job.

After your application has been accepted, you should be able to sign any final paperwork by mail, but you might need to prove your income or employment status with a paycheck, tax return, or offer letter.

Review the lease carefully before signing and make sure you understand your responsibilities and the landlord's responsibilities.

Think through your lease terms—do you want to lock in your lease, or would you rather have flexibility to leave after six months? In different places, different types of leases might be common. For example, a college town might only have annual leases that are coordinated with the school year, while month-to-month terms might be possible in other cities. When you sign your lease, you might have to send the first month's rent and an additional deposit via cashier's check rather than personal check and some of this money might be non-refundable.

> ### MY EXPERIENCE
>
> *Try to research the requirements in your area for signing a lease. Friends of ours who moved overseas struggled to sign a lease because they had no history of income in the country where they wanted to live.*

For Buying: Mortgage, Inspection, and Closing

If you want to buy, there are a number of strategies. Some people prefer to work through an agent or a mortgage lender and others don't. These suggestions are just that, suggestions, whose applicability will vary based on your situation.

Buying a home is more complicated and higher-stakes than renting, so be careful throughout the process. Talk with others who have done it before or look online for help. Consider involving an attorney to advise on any necessary documents.

Logistical Considerations

When you do find the home that seems to be the one, *try to conceal your excitement* so that you can remain in a good position for negotiating. Make sure you feel satisfied that you know as much about the property and the area as you can before submitting an offer.

Do your homework before bidding and provide an opening bid based on similar prices. Home buying requires a negotiation process, so you don't necessarily want to offer what they're asking, unless their request is lower than similar houses that have been sold or the market is very competitive.

Depending on economic conditions, you might be able to negotiate a better deal, such as having the seller pay part of the closing costs or leave something behind for you, like the appliances or a piece of furniture that catches your eye.

You'll also have to settle on whether you will be the sole owner or if your partner will share ownership.

Mortgage Options

Your credit score is a big factor in the terms of your loan. Your score is based on your credit report, so request copies from the three credit bureaus (TransUnion, Experian, and Equifax) and make sure the reports are accurate. There are steps you can take to improve your credit score, like paying down any balances on your credit cards if you can afford to.

When you look for a mortgage, shop around. If you're willing to look for cheaper airfare or negotiate when buying a car, then it's worth your time to try to find a better deal for one of the biggest financial commitments of your life.

The most significant number is the annual percentage rate (APR), but banks price loans differently, so request an initial fees worksheet with your mortgage offer. The rates on this sheet are not guaranteed, but should help you in comparing lenders. The lender may be willing to reduce some of the fees in order to get your business—you'll just have to ask.

A number of different types of loans are available to you aside from the standard 30-year mortgage. First, choose whether you'll want a fixed-rate mortgage or an adjustable-rate mortgage (ARM). There are also hybrid ARMs where the interest rate is fixed for the first several years of the loan. ARM mortgages have less-predictable monthly payments, but often, a lower initial interest rate and can be advantageous if you're planning to sell your home well before you pay off your mortgage.

Government-backed loans, such as Federal Housing Administration (FHA) loans, often have less stringent credit and down payment requirements.

If you can't afford 20% for a down payment, you can obtain private mortgage insurance to help you get a loan with a smaller down payment. You can also borrow up to $50,000 from your 401(k) plan for any purpose, depending on the rules of your plan.

Once you've found a lender, you can apply to be *pre-approved*. Pre-approval will let you know how much a lender will be willing to pay for your new home and will let realtors know you're serious. This is different from being *pre-qualified*, which is a quick review of your finances. Being pre-qualified can also help your bargaining power and help identify problems with your credit.

Inspection and Agreement

A home inspection is an important part of the process. A certified home inspector can tell you if there are any repairs or deferred maintenance on the home. A local inspector should be familiar with the types of problems common to homes in that part of the country, such as problems with mold, termites, or the foundation. The inspector will go over the whole house and tell you whether there are any major conditions that should scare you away or give you leverage when negotiating the final price.

A title inspection can tell you if there are any title defects that affect the status of the property, such as a lien or property restriction.

You will also need to line up home insurance. If you are serious about a specific place, contact a few insurers to get quotes from them.

The insurance value is based on the cost of rebuilding the house. It also covers a percentage of the valuables inside (75% is typical) with usual coverage maximums for certain things like jewelry or artwork.

You will also need to choose a deductible. A higher deductible will give you a lower monthly rate, though you need to keep enough money on hand so you can cover the deductible if you do need to file a claim.

Provide the lender's contact information to the home insurance company you've chosen.

Closing

After you submit an offer and agree to purchase a property, draw up a purchase agreement with a closing date (usually within 6–8 weeks). Things can go wrong before the closing date, so wait until you have closed before you commit too heavily to setting a move-in date.

Have your lawyer or agent review the deal, as there should be some contingency clauses in case you're not able to get a mortgage or if the inspection hasn't been completed and problems are found during the inspection. Send the signed purchase agreement to your loan officer promptly. Make sure he or she has everything needed to approve the loan and be in constant contact.

Your lender will update the loan amount and other details accordingly and provide you with more details, including a Good Faith Estimate. The Good Faith Estimate is a regulatory document that lists all the fees and costs for the mortgage—like appraisal fees, origination fees, processing fees, underwriting fees, and credit report fees. The costs on the Good Faith Estimate should match what you saw on the initial fees Worksheet. If any fees are different, ask your loan officer to correct it. If he or she won't, then you might want to go with a different lender. Your lender will also provide a HUD Settlement Statement that lists all the charges you will pay at closing, including title insurance in case the seller doesn't actually own the property.

The closing varies by location but is usually anticlimactic. You'll have to sign a stack of papers and there will be a notary, your lender, your realtor, and possibly real estate attorneys. Make sure you have funds in the form of a cashier's check or money wire—not a personal checkbook.

Alternatively, it's possible to close on your home remotely, without being there in person. You could sign the documents in advance or empower an attorney to sign documents on your behalf. You would likely need to send funds in advance.

• • •

Whether renting or buying, choosing your home brings your dreams one step closer to reality.

9 Arrange Your Move

Once you have lined up your job and a place to live, the next big task to tackle is how to get all your stuff there. For many people, the physical act of moving belongings is the least pleasant part of the whole process. But actually moving *yourself* there can be the most fun.

Let's look at the options for you to arrange to move your things, your pets, and yourself to your new place.

PLANNING TO MOVE YOURSELF AND YOUR THINGS

Step-by-Step Plan

	STEP	HOW LONG TO START BEFORE MOVE	DURATION
PLANNING HOW YOU'LL MOVE			
	Possessions	**6–20 weeks**	**1–16 weeks**
1.	Determine how to move your things		
2.	Get estimates from movers		
3.	Schedule move with movers		
	People	**6–20 weeks**	**1–18 weeks**
4.	Decide how to move yourself		
5.	Decide how to move your pets		
6.	Make arrangements		

Budgeting

There can be a significant difference in costs between the various options for moving your things. My estimates are intended to give you a range of potential costs. The low budget estimate is based on a move of a one-bedroom home over a distance of a few hundred miles; the high budget estimate is based on moving a home with several bedrooms over a thousand miles. Costs will vary depending on how you choose to move; these options are outlined to help you determine the best one for you.

Low budget estimate: $450
If you don't have to purchase packing supplies and can drive to your new home within a day, costs may be quite low.

Mid budget estimate: $4,500
If you hire movers and have a long trip to move yourself and want to do some sightseeing on the way, costs will be a little higher.

High budget estimate: $12,500
Hiring full-service movers and making a vacation out of your relocation can lead to substantial costs.

Example Expenses

EXPENSE	LOW ESTIMATE (DOLLARS)	MEDIUM ESTIMATE (DOLLARS)	HIGH ESTIMATE (DOLLARS)
OPTIONS FOR MOVING YOUR THINGS			
Load them in your car	5	100	500
Rent a truck	500	2,000	4,000
Move by cube	1,000	4,000	8,000
Hire movers	1,200	3,500	9,000
Hire full-service movers	3,000	8,000	15,000
Leave your things in storage	50 per month	100 per month	200 per month
Travel with some of your things	25	100	200
Ship them	50	200	1,000
Ship your car	600	1,000	2,000
EXAMPLE EXPENSES FOR MOVING YOURSELF			
Transportation expenses (e.g., plane ticket or gasoline)	50	300	2,000
Hotel nights on the way	0	300	3,000
Food on the way	40	300	2,000
Supplies for moving your pet	50	100	500

DETERMINING HOW TO MOVE YOUR THINGS

The options available will vary depending on how far you're moving, what you want to pay for, and how strong your friends' backs are. Your possessions may go a different route than you go yourself.

Regardless of how you arrange to have your things moved, keep a list of potential moving help with names and phone numbers, including friends and professional movers.

Here are some of the most common options; you might combine methods to minimize expenses and maximize convenience:

Load Things in Your Car

Put everything that fits into the back of your station wagon and hit the road. If it doesn't fit, give it away; if you really need it, you can buy a new one later.

PROS

- This is the least expensive option.

- It could be the least hassle and give you the most independence.

CONS

- Most Americans over 30 would need a pretty big station wagon to fit everything they want to keep.

- If you have to get rid of a lot of things for lack of hauling space, the cost and inconvenience of replacing all those things can be more work and expense. If so, consider choosing a different way to move your things.

Rent a Truck or Trailer

Go to the local truck rental and take care of it all yourself. You can tow your vehicle with you if you rent a dolly or trailer so that the drive wheels aren't on the ground. Or, if your vehicle is capable of towing, tow a trailer. Alternatively, if there are two of you moving, one of you could drive the moving truck and the other could drive the car.

PROS

- This is typically more cost-effective than hiring movers, and your carrying capacity is greater than a single vehicle's.

- Getting help from family or friends to load your moving truck can be the last opportunity (for a while) to bring everyone together.

CONS

- You'll probably need a few willing friends or family members to help load *and unload* everything.

- The likelihood of cargo getting broken en route is greater than with professional movers (and damages won't be insured).

- Driving a truck long-distance and parking in hotel parking lots can turn into more work than you'd expect.

- Be sure to estimate costs carefully, as gas and insurance prices will cut into any amount you hope to save by not hiring movers.

- There is a possibility of a road accident if you're not used to driving a moving truck or towing a trailer.

Move by Cube or Pod

A company delivers a large box or "pod" to your current residence, which you load over the period of a few days. Once you're done, the pod is picked up and delivered to your new residence, where you unload it.

PROS

- This option gives you more time to load everything than if you rent a truck.

- A pod can be cheaper than hiring movers.

- Some of the pods are large—with even enough room to move a small car.

- You have flexibility with a pod. You could hire a mover to do the unloading for you, or you can arrange to have the pod left at your new home for several days until you're able to unload it completely.

CONS

- Finding a place to store a pod while you're packing it can be difficult in a city or in a neighborhood with strict ordinances.

- Inside the pod, large items can move and cause damage in transit. Without experience, you might not know how to tie things down securely.

Hire Movers to Move Your Stuff

Why do all the lifting if someone else can do it for you?

PROS

- Leave the heavy lifting to people who have the tools, strength, and experience.

- Any damages are mostly insured.
- You can tell the movers where to place things in your new home rather than trying to place them there yourself.

CONS

- This option obviously costs more than doing it yourself.
- Your stuff could take longer to arrive at your new home than you will.
- You still need to pack everything in boxes yourself.

Hire Movers to Pack and Move Your Stuff

Why do anything yourself that you can get someone else to do for you?

PROS

- This option demands the least physical effort from you. It can be very helpful if you can afford it.
- You can still organize what types of effects are grouped together for packing and develop a system of coding boxes (as they are packed) so that the most needed items can be unpacked first.
- Your belongings can be insured against damage.

CONS

- This is much more expensive than having movers just move your boxes.
- You have to be comfortable relying on someone else, albeit a professional, to package your items securely.

Leave It Behind in Storage

Why even move it when you can just store it?

PROS

- Storage allows you to hold onto things that you won't need in the new place or don't have room for anymore.
- This option lightens your load and can decrease up-front moving costs.

CONS

- If you're going to move far away, you won't be able to access your storage space easily.

- Add the ongoing rent of storage space to your regular expenses.

- The more you move something, the higher the risk it will be damaged, so moving things in and out of storage causes more wear and tear than just moving them directly to your new place.

Take It While Traveling

Take a plane, train, or bus to your new home and bring what you can with you.

PROS

- While many airlines charge for checked bags, look for the best deal and you might be able to save some moving costs, especially if you can move your essentials by plane and leave the rest behind.

- This might be the best option for an overseas move.

CONS

- Airline bag fees mean that this won't be free.

- If this is your only means of moving things, you will be very limited in what you can take with you.

Ship Stuff

Send things via a shipping agency or by aircraft cargo.

PROS

- This can be a quicker way to send things than by moving truck.

- Books can be shipped at a low "Media Mail" rate through the United States Postal Service.

- This can be the most convenient option for international moves.

CONS

- Shipping is not cost effective for sending a large volume of things or heavy things.

Move by Boat

The days of moving overseas by ship are not over; you can still pack your suitcases and take things with you.

PROS

- You can enjoy a memorable voyage in your transition between old and new homes.

- If you wish to avoid air travel and would rather not be separated from your things, this is a good way to move overseas.

CONS

- This can be a long and expensive journey.

Ship Your Car or Motorcycle

You can ship your vehicle too so that you don't have to drive it. But first be sure that your vehicle will be appropriate for your destination. For overseas moves, it will probably be more cost-effective to sell your car before you leave and buy another one if you need it where you're going.

PROS

- If you don't want to go on a long road trip or have multiple cars to move, this can be a necessity.

CONS

- Work out the numbers: it can be cheaper to sell your car and buy one in your new home.

- This is not a good value if you will sell your car within the next couple years.

- This is usually done by a moving company that specializes in vehicle moves, so you'll have to coordinate logistics with another mover.

- The vehicle moving industry does more work with other businesses (like car dealerships) and is not as geared towards the individual consumer.

- State regulations can vary. Just because your car passes your state's emission inspection doesn't mean that it will pass the inspection in your new state.

LINING UP A MOVING PLAN

Finding a Mover

If you do decide to hire movers, the process isn't as simple as you'd think. There are many movers out there with different specialties. Most relocations are happening *within* a city, so the majority of the moving companies are local movers.

When to Move

If you plan to use a moving company, you'll probably want to contact them as soon as you land a job. If you've already set a start date at work, your move date may not be very flexible, but realize that the timing of your move can affect its cost.

To recruit friends or family to help you move, find out when people won't be available and try to schedule your move date accordingly.

According to U-Haul, 45% of moves happen between Memorial Day and Labor Day. If you're moving children, you might not have a choice but to move during that window. If you can move at the beginning of summer, children might participate in a summer camp in your new town and have a chance to meet new friends before school starts. Summertime and month-end moves are much more popular—and therefore more expensive and more difficult to schedule. If you're moving in the summer, you should start this process at least two months in advance.

If you do have a choice about the time of year, research the weather conditions along the way to and at your new hometown. Moving in the winter can be cheaper, but icy or even closed roadways can cause delays.

Multiple Movers Involved

The moving company might seem to be a single entity to you, but the company will often engage with multiple independent organizations (also known as subcontracting) to move your things across a long distance. There are thousands of independently owned and operated moving agencies throughout the country. These moving agencies are distinct companies in themselves but may have an affiliation with a nationwide moving brand. Here are the various moving agents who could be involved in your move:

- **Booking agent:** Comes to your home to estimate what your move will cost and schedules the moving date with you.

147

- **Origin agent:** Arrives on moving day to load up your things and may also pack your boxes. This is often the same as the booking agent.

- **Hauling agent:** Transports your household goods the many miles to your new home. The hauling agent can also be the same as your origin agent.

- **Destination agent:** Delivers your things to your new home.

For any movers you are in contact with, find out which additional agents they use so that you can vet them independently.

Getting Quotes

For a cross-country move, moving services are usually priced based on the total weight of things being moved. International movers sometimes assess fees based on cubic space. For a local move, costs are usually hourly. There are also usually additional fees added to either pricing structure—for additional services like wrapping furniture, or for challenges in the moving process—like stairs or having to use special equipment on awkward items.

There are three basic types of estimates: binding, non-binding, and not-to-exceed estimates.

A *non-binding estimate* is just that: an estimate; your final costs might be lower or higher by up to 10%. A *binding estimate* is usually more thorough and guarantees a final moving cost except for any other fees.

A *not-to-exceed estimate* is sometimes called a price-protected estimate. It means that even if your items weigh more than estimated, you still won't pay more than the estimate. The difference from a binding estimate is that if your shipment is lighter than estimated, you will pay less—whatever the actual costs are. So, a not-to-exceed estimate represents the most you will pay (except for any other fees) and your actual costs could be less.

Contact movers to have them take an inventory for you. A booking agent will come and see what you have and give you an estimate based on the weight of your goods, the distance being moved, and any packing materials or services you need them to provide. This is an opportunity to ask any questions.

It's a good idea to have three to five different companies come out to survey your home. When the estimators come in, make sure they see all the rooms and closets and account for everything, and that they make note of any antique or fragile items. It's also helpful if you have already gotten rid of things that you don't plan to move (or at least point them out so they are not included in the estimate). If you buy a new couch after your estimate is done, or if you forget to show them what's in your attic, your moving bill will be higher than the estimate, and the movers may consider a binding estimate invalid.

Also, know what additional fees the movers charge so that you're not caught off guard. If you are moving appliances, ask whether the movers charge to disconnect and move your appliances. Be sure to ask how long it will take for your things to arrive.

Some moving companies offer a discount if you are a member of certain organizations like AARP or AAA. However, price isn't the only criteria. Some provide a higher level of service, have more lenient policies, or have been in business for a longer period of time.

It's a good idea to find out ahead of time if movers can park their large truck near your current home and also your next home.

> ## MY EXPERIENCE
>
> *Once we chose our movers, they asked me if they could bring their 18-wheeler into our apartment complex. The roads inside the complex looked wide enough, so I said yes. But on moving day, the apartment manager came out and refused to let them in, so they had to go back and get a smaller truck. They said they would have to charge me extra for it, but perhaps because of a well-timed cash tip, that charge didn't show up on the final invoice.*

Screening

Letting someone else take care of all your worldly possessions can be difficult, so you want to make sure that you trust them.

You might not be able to find a spotless mover, but moving is a high-stakes game. The fact is that movers are people and people make mistakes. Combine that with the fact that bad things sometimes happen to good people, and that's how you can end up with hundreds of online reviews that the moving industry wouldn't be proud of.

However, you can use these resources to determine whether your movers, including the origin agent, hauling agent, and destination agent, are good to work with:

- **FMCSA Registration:** All movers should be registered with the Federal Motor Carrier Safety Administration (see www.protectyourmove.gov). Request their USDOT number or MC/MX number to look up their information on the Government's Safety and Fitness Electronic Records (SAFER) System. This will provide you with a history of inspections and crashes and tell you whether a company is authorized to operate.

- **BBB:** The Better Business Bureau tracks complaints and status of companies. Complaints can vary from rudeness to breaking things to outright deception. Companies that do more work will have more complaints, so *how the company responds to complaints* is important. Also, watch out for movers that have no complaints against them; this could indicate that they have recently changed names to escape a history of complaints or that they're brand new and have limited experience.

  o **BBB Rating:** The BBB provides a rating from A+ to F based on the length of time the business has been in operation, the history of complaints filed, having the proper licensing, and other factors.

  o **BBB Accreditation:** This is a voluntary program that member agents choose to pay for. Accredited businesses meet the BBB's criteria for making a good faith effort to resolve complaints.

- **AMSA Membership:** The American Moving and Storage Association screens movers and requires them to uphold a code of ethics. AMSA has a list of current members: visit www.moving.org/promovers_az.asp or call them at 1-888-849-2672.

- **AMSA Pro Mover program:** An additional quality certification program, this includes annual background checks.

- **RIM Certification:** The Registered International Mover program has established standards for professionalism and ethics: www.promover.org/rim_intl

- **Ask questions:** When you talk to them on the phone or when they come to estimate your move, ask how long they've been in business and what their policies and charges are. Make sure to get any policies or guarantees in writing.

- **Ask for recommendations**: Most movers are happy to provide you with letters from satisfied customers. Contact some references and ask them how careful, reliable, and professional the mover was.

- **Review government literature**: The government provides two publications: *Ready to Move?* (available at www.protectyourmove.gov/documents/ReadyToMove-2006-april.pdf) and *Your Rights and Responsibilities When You Move* (available at www.protectyourmove.gov/documents/Rights-and-Responsibilities-2013.pdf) which outline your rights and empower you to make a responsible selection in movers.

- **Beware of red flags:** You shouldn't have to pay a cash deposit prior to the move, the mover should not provide an estimate for moving your goods sight unseen, and the company should have a local address (not just a PO Box). Their location should look like a legitimate professional business and their license information should be readily available. Also be leery of movers whose estimate is significantly lower than the others and who have a very generic name. Do not sign any blank or incomplete documents.

Insurance

Homeowners' insurance may cover some moving insurance expenses. Here are some standard coverage options available to you through the moving company:

- **"Released value" coverage:** Often provided by movers as standard, this will reimburse you for damaged goods based on the weight of the goods that are damaged at a rate of about 60 cents per pound. The rate at which they will provide reimbursement is low, so repayment for any small goods that are damaged could be much less than the items are worth.

- **Separate liability insurance:** You can also buy separate insurance through the moving company. This coverage would pay for the cost to *replace* or *repair* any lost or damaged item that isn't covered under the released value coverage.

- **Full replacement value protection insurance:** This would require the mover to repair, replace, or pay for any broken or lost items. The amount paid would be equal to the cost to repair the item or to buy a similar item. Movers can limit their liability for damage to high-value items like china, jewelry, and antiques.

Finding a Vehicle Mover

If you decide to use a car transporter, check with your auto insurance company to see if any damage incurred in transit will be covered.

To ship your vehicle, work with a carrier or a broker. A *carrier* is the company that moves the vehicle, and a *broker* is a third party who makes arrangements with a carrier on your behalf. Carriers will often give priority to car dealers who are moving many vehicles at once. Brokers can be slightly more expensive, but they know the reputable carriers and will be able to contact several to get you the best price and schedule. Brokers can also help you out if there is an issue with the carrier.

As with choosing a regular moving company, you can also use the FMCSA and BBB to select reliable auto transport. Find out what kind of insurance they provide, whether your car will travel enclosed or exposed, and where exactly they'll deliver it, as some will only deliver to a central terminal in your area.

Finding Storage

If you're going to put some things in storage, look for surveillance cameras, fences, and other security measures. If you're storing wood, musical instruments, or artwork, look for climate-controlled storage. Get the right size space for your stuff—not too big, but not too small. Check to see when you can access your unit and how easily you can get things into it. When you visit and walk into a unit, does it smell okay, and is it clean and dry? Can you have your monthly payment made automatically? Are there hand trucks and dollies available to use?

Once you choose a place, make and keep an inventory of everything you store. Pack and seal your boxes and don't stack them too high where they could fall. If you're going to share storage space with someone, make sure you can trust them. Since you'll be out of the area, you might want to authorize someone to access your storage space on your behalf if needed. And last, but not least, get a good quality lock.

Moving Truck Coverage

Most auto insurance will cover you driving a rental car. But because a rental truck is a substantially bigger and more expensive vehicle that can cause more damage, neither personal car insurance nor credit cards typically cover a rental truck. Check to make sure you're covered or purchase additional coverage from the moving company.

Your approach to insurance and additional protection for your moving truck will reflect your general perspective on insurance. In actuality, you probably won't need insurance, and companies do make money on it. But if you don't have insurance or coverage for your truck, the risks can be substantial, even to the point of bankruptcy. So make sure you are protected. Having a higher deductible, if you have the option, will decrease your cost, but you will have to pay out of pocket if there is a claim.

Here are the types of coverage that are likely to be offered at the rental counter:

- **Limited damage waiver**: With this coverage, the rental company waives its right to make you pay for a collision or loss of the vehicle. There could still be a deductible for this that you would have to pay for damage. This relieves you of any financial responsibility should any damage occur to the truck or towing equipment. This coverage is not valid if you are using the equipment in a way that violates the rental agreement, such as taking it off-road or running drugs with it. If you do not purchase this coverage, you will be responsible to pay for any damage to the vehicle, as well as paying the rental company for the amount of time that the vehicle is being repaired and out of service.

- **Personal medical and life coverage**: This option offers medical coverage to the truck driver and passengers and covers any costs in excess of your personal insurance coverage. It also provides you and your passengers with life coverage in the case of a fatality.

- **Supplemental liability insurance**: Liability insurance protects you and the rental company if you hit something or someone while driving the rental truck and are at fault. The rental company is required to have liability insurance for its trucks, but there is a maximum value. In the event of a major collision, this maximum could be exceeded, so supplemental coverage provides a higher maximum limit, typically $1,000,000 or less.

- **Cargo insurance**: This coverage will reimburse you for damage to your possessions in the truck due to a collision or disaster. There are a number of items that will not be covered, like currency, firearms, cell phones, and many other things. And many types of damage are typically excluded, including damage caused by insects, theft, failing to pack items securely, and war.

- **Towing insurance**: This covers any damage to your vehicle if you will be towing it with your rental truck. There is a deductible and exclusions as well, similar to cargo insurance.

DETERMINING HOW TO MOVE YOURSELF

If planning how to move your things can be one of the most draining parts of relocating, then planning how to move yourself can be one of the most fun, especially if you can make a vacation out of it.

You can also move just as you'd travel normally and fly, take a train, or ride a bus. Taking a bus could be the cheapest but possibly slowest option. Booking a flight at least six weeks in advance will help lower the cost of the flight.

If your possessions are traveling separately from you, think about taking the opportunity to visit other destinations en route to your new place. If it will take two weeks for your belongings to make it across the country, why not spend those two weeks touring Europe and then show up in your new place in time to meet your stuff?

Road Trip Option

If you can afford to take a few days to travel, hop in your car and take a road trip across the country. This is a great idea if you do not have very young children. Whether you're moving from Columbus to Chicago or Pensacola to Portland (Maine or Oregon), there will be things along the way worth seeing. If nothing else, driving to your new home may make you realize how far away you're going and help you appreciate the changing landscape.

In planning a road trip, prepare for the weather. If you're charting a drive through the upper Midwest in the middle of winter or will pass through Florida during hurricane season, anticipate altering your route if necessary.

Be aware that some states have restrictions on what you can bring across state lines. For example, California and Florida limit the types of fresh fruit that enter the state.

You could camp out along the way, stay at roadside motels, or find luxury accommodations. If you're driving a moving truck, you may want to avoid big cities, even if it means a longer drive. It can be hard to find parking and drive around in cities, so you might prefer to stay in rural areas along the highway. It would be prudent to call motels ahead of time and make sure that they have room for you to park.

To be proactive about your road trip, check to see if your phone service provider has coverage along the way, and keep a written list of emergency contacts in case your phone doesn't work and you have to stop somewhere to make a call.

Try to have fun! You could create a music shuffle with songs that were written about or by artists from your new home. Play road trip bingo, look for license plates, or have passengers count the animals on their side of the road. Take pictures of funny signs or places you're staying and post them online if you have an Internet connection. Pick up post cards from every town you pass through or stay in and mail them back home.

On your way, give yourself time to unwind which includes some time doing interesting things out of the car. If you pull a driving marathon, you might arrive at your new place too tired and sore to unpack and appreciate that you've finally made it.

> ## MY EXPERIENCE
>
> *We decided to make a nice road trip of our journey to Seattle, stopping at places along the way that appealed to us. We moved in February, so we tried to avoid driving through snowy mountain passes. We charted a route that took us through some of the places we were most interested in between our old home and our new one.*
>
> *Visiting the Grand Canyon and Las Vegas along the way was a vacation in itself and helped make our relocation a more special experience.*

International Move

If you're making an international move, the rules get more complicated. Check the immigration laws of your destination country as there will likely be rules about health, employment, and criminal activity before you can be admitted. You need a valid passport and possibly a visa. Find out what type of driving permit you will need. Your destination country might also require inoculations that may have to be started several months before moving. It's much easier to relocate through an employer than to go it alone.

The de-facto way to move overseas is by air travel, which is usually the cheaper way to move yourself, though taking a trip by boat can be viable as well. Here are some ways you could take a transatlantic or transpacific journey by boat:

- **Cruise ship**: *Repositioning voyages,* or cruises where the ship is relocating from serving the Americas to serving Europe, could be a great one-way option. These cruises usually have a lower cost per day and have fewer entertainment options than typical cruises. However, like a typical cruise, there will be multiple ports of call where you can get off the boat. These trips can take from two weeks to a month.

- **Ocean liner or yacht:** These elegant vessels will provide you a luxurious experience on your journey. Travel time can range from just over a week to a month.

- **Freightliner:** Traveling on a cargo ship isn't as glamorous, but it is a cheaper and more unique experience. These ships book six to ten passengers to go overseas with the captain and crew. The boats include guest bedrooms and private bathrooms with shared laundry, dining, and exercise facilities. You might, however, be without many modern conveniences like elevators, Internet access, and stabilizers that prevent the boat from rocking in the ocean, so watch out if you're prone to seasickness. The duration for one of these voyages is more variable and depends on how many stops are scheduled along the way.

Transportation Logistics

Once you've determined how to move yourself and your things, you can make an itinerary to share with friends and family. At the very least, it will help you keep track of key details of your relocation.

Let people know of your schedule and itinerary and agree on times to check in.

As you're planning your move, factor in what you'll do after your stuff is picked up by the movers. Will you leave right away, get a hotel for your last night in town, stay with a friend, or sleep on the floor in your empty home? Will you arrive at your new home before your stuff arrives—or try to arrive at the same time?

If there's a period of time at either end of your journey when you'll be without your possessions, keep some key things on hand that you'll need. If you have children, make it fun for them by treating it like an indoor camping trip. If you're staying with relatives or friends, you don't want to overstay your welcome.

ARRANGING TO MOVE YOUR PETS

Moving with a pet can be tricky. Ask yourself whether moving the pet is in its best interest based on its age and ability to handle stress. Perhaps leaving your pet behind with a friend or relative could be a viable option; you could visit your pet on visits back to the area. Or you could consider boarding your pet temporarily until you work out the details of moving it safely.

If you're moving overseas or to Hawaii, there might be quarantine procedures that could keep your pet isolated for 30 days or more. There could also be fees or dog breed restrictions; check with the consulate to inquire about the quality of the quarantine facilities and whether you'll be able to visit.

If you're interested, look into companies that can help you navigate the regulations that animals are subject to and take care of logistics for you.

Before you move, check with your veterinarian for any recommended emergency supplies that you should have on hand. Moving a bird or snake between states might require a health certificate from your veterinarian no more than ten days prior to traveling. Check with the Veterinarian's Office or State Department of Agriculture to find the applicable laws in your destination state.

Bus and train companies typically only allow service animals, so taking your pet is not an option with them.

Regardless of how you move your animal, make sure to have the right kind of carrier. Airlines have policies on what types of carriers are allowed; for example, birds need to be in a plastic crate, not a metal cage. For other animals, choose a large enough size and expose your pet to it in advance.

Driving

If you'll be driving to your destination, some hotels and many motels will accept pets, but call and confirm before making a reservation (as online information could be out of date).

If your pet isn't used to traveling in a vehicle, take it on short rides before the trip. You might want to reward your pet with a treat after each drive.

Flying

It's possible to have your pet checked as baggage or to ship your pet as cargo, but the Humane Society regards this as a last resort. The experience is very stressful for animals. Some animals have a heightened risk of respiratory trouble during this type of travel, and there is a risk of death due to rough handling or lack of oxygen.

For an additional fee, you can bring your pet in a carrier that fits under your seat as long as your pet has enough room inside to move around. When bringing a pet on board with you, you will have to take the pet out of the crate and carry it through the security screening. This probably won't be a very enjoyable experience for you or your pet. Read your airline's pet travel web page for other restrictions.

Shipping

Some animals can be shipped via a shipping company. Before shipping an animal, read additional guides, consult with your vet, and check the rules of the shipping company. Some companies will not ship certain animals. Mammals and birds are usually not allowed to be mailed, though poultry and fowl are allowed. Non-poisonous bugs, like bees, butterflies, and ladybugs can sometimes be mailed. Certain types of reptiles and amphibians will only be mailed by certain carriers.

Animals should be shipped overnight, and in case something goes wrong, you should ship on a Monday or Tuesday so that the animal isn't stuck in a warehouse over the weekend. Also check the weather in your destination city as you don't want a pet to be exposed to extreme temperature.

When shipping an animal, it's important to use an appropriately sized and sturdy container. The boxes should be cushioned so that the animal is protected, but not boxed in too tightly for it to move. Small air holes should be made in the box and some moisture inside the box may be appropriate, depending on the animal.

Your pet should be in good health, though depending on the type of animal, it's often recommended not to feed it for at least a day before shipping it.

• • •

Arranging to move all these things with you can be quite a logistical challenge, but these steps are some of the last ones before making the *big move*.

10 Say Goodbye

If your action steps have been following along with the book, some of the hardest tasks are out of the way. You know where you're going and how you're going to get there. You know where you'll work, where you'll live, and how your stuff is going to get there.

The next tasks to accomplish are generally simpler, but there are quite a few—with tons of details.

PLANNING TO SAY GOODBYE

Step-by-Step Plan

	STEP	HOW LONG TO START BEFORE MOVE	DURATION
SAYING GOODBYE			
1.	Sell your home	8–39 weeks	6–39 weeks
2.	Pare down your possessions	12–26 weeks	2–26 weeks
3.	Take care of the details	4–25 weeks	4–25 weeks
4.	Let people know	2–6 weeks	1–6 weeks

Budgeting

If you normally have a personal budget, it would be a good idea to re-budget once you know what your annual income will be as well as your home costs. This annual budget could help you make sure that you don't sign up for too large of a TV and Internet package for your income at your new place.

Low budget estimate: $1,590
If you're able to make money by selling some possessions, retrieving your rental deposit, and receiving some cash gifts as going-away presents, you could even come out ahead during this part of your moving process.

Mid budget estimate: $17,740
Taking care of final visits to the doctor, the vet, and the car mechanic could cost you. Cleaning services before moving out of your old place plus application fees and set-up fees at your new home will add up.

High budget estimate: $55,300
Visiting the doctor, vet, and car mechanic could uncover problems that need to be addressed before you move, and closing costs on selling your home could be substantial. These expenses are hard to predict.

Example Expenses

EXPENSE	LOW ESTIMATE (DOLLARS)	MEDIUM ESTIMATE (DOLLARS)	HIGH ESTIMATE (DOLLARS)
PARE DOWN YOUR POSSESSIONS			
Costs to get rid of your things	0	50	500
Income from selling your things	-2,000	-200	0
SELL YOUR HOME			
Home inspection	250	400	800
Painting and decorating	0	100	1,000
Home closing costs Can vary significantly depending on what portion of costs are paid by buyer.	5,000	15,000	35,000
Capital gains taxes Depends on whether your home has appreciated in value. A loss in value can reduce your tax burden.	-500	2,000	15,000
CLOSE OUT CURRENT OBLIGATIONS			
Doctor visits	0	20	300
Vet trips	20	50	500
Car mechanic inspection	20	200	1,000
Clean	0	200	500
Returned deposits	-1,000	-200	0
PREPARE FOR YOUR NEW HOME			
One-time fees to set up new utilities and new services	0	50	300
School applications	0	20	200

Expense	Low Estimate (Dollars)	Medium Estimate (Dollars)	High Estimate (Dollars)
Let people know			
Goodbye activities (e.g., party, dinners)	0	100	200
Goodbye gifts	-200	-50	0
Total	**1,590**	**17,740**	**55,300**

Selling Your Home

Selling your home is very similar to purchasing a home as explained in Chapter 8, but you're in a different role.

Options for Selling

If you have a home to sell, you have two basic options: get a realtor (seller's agent) or try to do it yourself.

A realtor can help protect you from legal liability, provide negotiation skills, and has professional contacts to help close deals faster.

Selling the house yourself can save you money, but it might not be a feasible option if you relocate before your house sells. For Sale by Owner (FSBO) web sites help you navigate this process without a realtor and list your home for sale.

Evaluating Your Home

To get an understanding of what your home will sell for, try to figure out how much your house is worth. You can look at other listings in your area, but look only at homes that are very similar. A realtor can help set a list price for your home, or you can schedule a professional appraisal to approximate the market value of your home.

The price people are willing to pay is dependent on a few factors, like the surrounding neighborhood, the convenience of where you are located, the size and amenities of your home, and the home's condition. Even if you have a very nice home, its market value can be diminished if other homes in the area aren't as nice.

While your home might be worth a lot to you, prospective buyers won't have the same feelings for it that you do. Some people viewing your home will be critical of it. It's hard to close a sale if you're hesitant to sell your home for less than you think it's worth. It's even harder when you're emotionally attached.

The process will be easier if you can dissociate yourself from your home; think of it more as a *commodity* that you need to sell rather than a place where you made so many memories.

Choosing a Realtor

If you choose to use a realtor, make your decision carefully. The advice in Chapter 8 about choosing a realtor for buying a home applies here as well. Gather information from online reviews and other references, and look for someone knowledgeable about and successful in the local housing market. Interview agents referred to you or those you have read about. Do you trust the person? Is he or she professional?

Ask what he or she recommends for a price. Does that agree with your homework? Find out what kind of marketing plan the realtor would have for your home, including advertising and open houses. An agent with experience selling houses like yours will price your home well.

Be clear with your expectations, such as who will be present for open houses, and set a schedule for communicating to make sure you stay connected and aren't left in the dark. Once you choose a realtor, keep track of all documentation such as emails, forms, and appraisals.

You will have to sign a listing agreement which is valid for a set amount of time, usually one to three months. You might be able to negotiate a lower commission fee if your house is expensive. Or you could offer an incentive fee to the realtor if the house is sold within 5% of your asking price within a certain time frame.

You should have a lawyer help you review bids and contracts, and be aware that you will need money on hand to pay the closing costs.

As with buying a home, there will be other parties involved, such as a title company to prepare the title and close the loan.

Tips to Prepare and Market Your Home

When selling your home, you can't get more money by making your neighborhood look nicer or affecting market conditions, but you can spruce up your home to earn a higher sale price. There are also ways to make the most out of selling your home if you're not using a realtor.

Organize, Clean, and Fix

- **Have a home inspection:** A smart buyer will do their own inspection, but you don't want to be surprised if they discover a plumbing issue or leaky roof. Be proactive and take care of issues in advance, or at least notify a prospective buyer if their inspection will turn up anything like that.

- **Clean:** Wipe up dust, scrub grime off flooring, pressure clean the driveway, and polish the kitchen to make the place sparkle. You could hire professional cleaners to do this for you.

- **Paint:** A fresh coat of paint on the walls can help them look clean. Choose a light and neutral paint color to make rooms seem larger and allow a buyer to imagine making the home theirs more easily without influence from your personal style.

- **Clear clutter:** Put away personal photos, knick-knacks, papers, or anything else so that the home looks less "lived-in." Buyers will want to see closets and any storage space, so now is a good time to clean out junk if you haven't already. Sell or store extra furniture so the home feels larger.

- **Let there be light:** Upgrade interior lights or add lighting so that your home is welcoming and easy to see.

- **Clean any smells:** Steam your carpet, throw out the trash, and make sure your home is ventilated.

- **Maintain and fix things:** Take care of bent blinds, bad floor tiles, ceiling leaks, and cabinet squeaks to make your home seem newer.

- **Check the curb appeal:** Replacing or repainting your mailbox and house numbers can be a relatively low cost way to make the home look newer. Trim the hedges and mow, fertilize, and water the yard or bring in a landscaper if you need more help.

- **Stage your home:** To go even further, you can hire a professional home stager or get a one-time consultation in order to arrange your home to look better to buyers.

- **Temporarily remove pets and children:** Offer potential buyers an undistracted visit while they view your home.

Selling on Your Own

Here are some tips to help you sell your home without the help of a realtor:

- **Take good photos**: Enlist a talented friend or hire a professional to take good photos of your home for the listing.

- **Advertise your home**: In addition to listing your home, advertise it via a newspaper, online classifieds, and with a sign in the yard.

- **Be available**: Buyers might move on to another home if they aren't able to see yours at their convenience.

- **Offer perks**: If you'd like to entice an interested buyer or need help closing the deal, offer to include the first year of home association dues, pay for part of the closing costs, or leave behind an amenity like a playground set, large TV, or some piece of furniture that the buyer commented on. A gift card for home improvement or services of a local handyman could help the sale close faster as well.

- **List below market value**: If you're eager to sell your home quickly, there are many individual investors as well as real estate investment firms who are willing to purchase homes quickly. You might have to drop your asking price, but it could be more lucrative than holding onto your home after you move. To do this, post an ad for your home and identify yourself as a motivated seller. If you live in a competitive housing market, listing your home under market value could stir interest and start a bidding war.

Other Options for Your Home

If you're not able to sell or if now isn't a good time to sell, look into these other options.

Lease out Your Home

Hire a property management company to help you rent out your home. They can recruit renters, run background checks on tenants, collect rent, and maintain your property. They typically charge between 5% and 20% of the rent for their services.

As with vetting a realtor, you'll want to screen potential property managers. Ask how many properties they manage, how often they will check on the property, how they handle maintenance, what the best way to contact them is, and how quickly you should expect them to respond to your calls or emails. Ask how you'll receive payment, whether you'll receive a monthly statement from them, and what they will do if they cannot collect the rent. You'll also want references, ideally from a homeowner like yourself.

Lease to Own

You could offer your property out to lease with an option to purchase. This could open your property up to people who don't have adequate credit history to qualify for a loan. A real estate agent can help you locate buyers who are interested in leasing to own. The lease period can be from six months to five years.

Corporate Housing

If you're having trouble finding a buyer, you could rent your home as furnished housing if you're willing to leave your furniture behind. You can usually charge more than you would make with traditional rentals and will be appealing to corporations or business travelers who need somewhere to stay for several months. Your home will be more appealing as a short-term rental if it's in a safe, convenient location and near businesses and transportation.

Vacation Rental

If your home is in a desirable location, you might be able to make it available for visiting vacationers if allowed by local laws. There are places online where you can list your residence, and you will also probably need to hire a service to keep the place clean. Just as with corporate housing, this will require you leaving your home furnished.

Keep It on the Market

If you're selling it yourself, you or your spouse could stay behind with the home for a few weeks until it sells, or have your realtor show your home for you. Having to pay for two homes can get costly, but if you're having difficulty finding the kind of offer you'd like, this option leaves the door open to sell the home at your asking price.

Short Sale or Deed-in-Lieu of Foreclosure

If your home is worth less than what you paid for it and you have little equity, you might want to enlist an attorney to help you through your options.

One possibility is to provide your lender with the deed to your property instead of having them foreclose—called *deed-in-lieu of foreclosure*. This option is less detrimental to your credit report than an actual foreclosure.

The bank might prefer a *short sale* arrangement, which also impacts your credit report, but it reduces the debt you owe and can mean that you won't owe anything to sell the home.

PARING DOWN YOUR POSSESSIONS

Many people believe that one of the main benefits of a move is the impetus to go through everything and get rid of extra junk that has amassed over the years. Are those things in your closet really important enough to be brought hundreds or thousands of miles to be put into another closet?

Reviewing Your Possessions

As you review your things, ask yourself if you've used an item recently and if you need to own it, or if you can rent, borrow, or improvise if you need it again.

If things are still in moving boxes from your last move, maybe you don't need to move them again. On the other hand, don't try to get rid of too much. You can cause some bad feelings and add stress to the process if other family members feel forced to part with things they want to keep. Moving a few too many items might be better than making someone throw away their childhood teddy bear.

Here are some things to keep in mind as you go through your home:

- Some things have sentimental value, but be realistic—You'll probably have a number of tough decisions to make during this process, and it might be time to admit that you can no longer justify keeping that life-size cardboard cutout of Stone Cold Steve Austin.

- Leave behind extra things you already have, like spare shoes, belts, pots, or bed sheets.

- If you have bulky or awkward items, you might sell those before you leave, such as sports boats, riding lawnmowers, or an extra freezer. For an overseas move, bringing appliances is expensive, and they might not be compatible with the electric current in your destination country.

- Dispose of things that you will accumulate in the future like plastic bags, glass jars, or small trinkets and decorations.

- Plants might not survive the journey, especially temperamental ones, so consider giving them away at your goodbye party.

- Go through your paper files. Bringing a file cabinet of old credit card statements might not be necessary, especially if you can access the information online or scan it to your computer.

- Consider what you'll need if you're moving to a new climate. A move from upstate New York to Tucson will require different clothing and household items. For instance, a yard with sand and rocks doesn't need a lawn mower.

- You could get rid of things and replace them once you get to your new home. The cost of buying new housewares may be offset by the savings and convenience of not transporting or storing them. If it's time to replace the contents of your underwear and sock drawer anyway, you can just buy new stuff when you arrive.

- Get an accurate floor plan of your new home. Measure your furniture so that you can draw where it will go and make sure it will fit.

- Know what you can't take. Movers won't move flammable, corrosive, or explosive items. So, give away or dispose of your paint thinner, varnish, oils, bleach, and fuel.

- As your moving date approaches, use up your food and dump or give away anything perishable. Toss opened flour, sugar, and other potentially messy items unless you can pack them in tightly sealed canisters or re-sealable plastic bags. Bring along snacks for your trip, but otherwise be prepared to buy takeout food at the end.

It's hard to do this all at once, so start small and spend 20 minutes per day going through less sentimental effects, like in the bathroom or kitchen. Just focus on one area at a time and sort items. You can make one pile for items to "get rid of," one pile for items to "keep," and one "maybe" pile to think about.

Ways to Get Rid of Things

Once you've identified what you're willing to part with, here are several ways to get rid of things or pass them on to someone else:

- **Yard or garage sale:** A sale is one way to off-load things and make a few bucks in the process. But temper your expectations; unless you're selling valuables, you might not make much money compared to the effort of running the garage sale.

- **Sell locally:** If you have furniture, lawn equipment, electronics, or smaller valuables to get rid of, post flyers in your apartment complex or neighborhood, advertise them in the newspaper, or use Craigslist to get people to come by and pick them up from you. If you want to get rid of stuff quickly, offer it for free.

- **Sell online:** If you're selling items that can be shipped, list them online on sites like Amazon or eBay. You could earn more money than with other methods, and you may have an easier time selling things that have a niche appeal. This will take effort on your part to package items and ship them out, or you could find a local service and pay them to take care of this for you.

- **Charity pick-up:** If you want to give away usable furniture, Goodwill, the Salvation Army, and other organizations are often willing to pick it up. You can call to schedule a pick-up time, and there are rules about what they will accept.

- **Deliver to charity or a re-seller:** If you have many things that don't have much value but are still usable, charities may be willing to take them. The Society for the Prevention of Cruelty to Animals will take sheets and towels. Hospitals or libraries may take books, or you could sell them to a used book retailer. Other things like clothes, housewares, and small electronics can be taken to Goodwill or Value Village, where they can be re-sold or otherwise redistributed. Check with the local food bank or shelter to see if they'll accept your non-perishable food.

- **Sell to a collector:** If you have valuable stamps, coins, or comics, look for a local collector or retailer willing to pay for them, rather than moving with them and potentially exposing them to damage.

- **Discard:** Some things just aren't valuable enough for further use. Depending on your local services, you might be able to recycle or compost items rather than sending them to a landfill.

- **Safely dispose:** Some things need to be disposed of in a special way. Fluorescent bulbs, computer electronics, and rechargeable batteries are examples of electronic waste that contains mercury—which can get into the water supply if improperly disposed of. Look for an e-waste disposal center for these items. Earth911.com at www.earth911.com has a search tool to help you find the nearest center.

- **Junk removal:** Some services will pick things up from your home for disposal.

- **Give to friends:** Set aside going-away gifts for special people. Give your friend that outfit that she complimented or that movie that you watched together. Give a buddy some of the games you've played together or some bottles from your liquor stash. As people come over in the weeks leading up to your move, have a pile of things that they are welcome to choose from. Hosting a moving party could be one way of getting people to come by and take some things from you.

- **Storage:** If you want to hold onto something or aren't ready to give it away, you can reserve a self-storage unit for it.

TAKING CARE OF THE DETAILS

As you prepare to leave, there are many loose ends to tie up.

Physical and Mental Preparation

- **Enjoy some last rituals:** Before moving away, do a few of the things you enjoy and reflect on your times here. Eat at your favorite restaurant, have a special evening at home with music and a bottle of wine, look through a scrapbook of memories, or do a few touristy things in town that you've never gotten around to.

- **Document it:** Take pictures or video of your home, both before and after you pack. Involve your children in making a keepsake book with photos of their favorite parts of the home where they can write down what they liked about each place.

- **Bring something local:** Identify some local food that your new place won't have. Whether that's smoked salmon, fry sauce, or Yuengling, bring some with you. You can share some with people you meet in your new place or enjoy it yourself.

- **Schedule your next trip back:** If you're leaving friends or family behind, they will want to know when you'll visit. If you can let them know you'll be back for the holidays, an upcoming wedding, or next summer, it will ease your saying goodbye.

- **Plan for your city:** Rent movies set in your future city, read online blogs, or follow social media personalities so that you can start learning the local culture of your new place. You can find more information sources in Chapter 4 and in the Online Resources section at the end of the book.

- **Prepare for changes to your routine:** Review what your daily routines might be like in the new place. How will these change from what you're used to now? Being aware of potential changes ahead of time makes for an easier transition.

- **Prepare for changes to your resources**: Moving may affect what resources you have available to you, such as money, time, and a personal support system. What resources might you gain in your new place?

- **Spend time with your children**: Make sure children understand (to the degree that they can) the details of what is happening. Reassure them that everything will be okay.

Take Care of Things

Make sure you take care of yourself, family, pets, and possessions before you go.

- **Go to the doctor**: Moving is stressful and involves physical labor, so you don't want a heart attack while moving your boxes. Visit your doctor and take care of any health issues that you've been wanting to address. Have your kids checked as well. Get proof that you and your family have received the latest immunizations, and get a hard copy of any standing prescriptions. You could request a copy of any medical records to take with you, or you can arrange to have them sent to a physician in your new town; however, your signature is required for either option. Could your doctor provide a referral to a medical practitioner in your new town?

- **Dental and eye care**: Be sure to get check-ups, any prescriptions, and copies of medical records.

- **Exercise**: It helps to be in good shape for all the work of moving: carrying a lot of stuff around, loading and unloading belongings, and even walking more than you might be used to.

- **Refill and transfer prescriptions**: You don't want to have to search for a pharmacy the day you arrive in your new area. Find out how your medications need to be stored so you can either keep them with you or leave them in your vehicle, if you're driving. If you will be moving overseas, find out if there is an equivalent medicine that you can purchase there, with or without a prescription.

- **Take your animals to the vet**: Make sure your pet is in good health and up to date on necessary vaccinations before you travel. Get any prescriptions refilled. If your pet is being shipped or traveling by air, you will need a signed proof of vaccination form within a few days prior to travel.

- **Car care:** If you're driving or having your car shipped, be sure to service your car before you leave. Some car service joints will inspect your car as part of an oil change. If you'll be driving a long distance, tell the mechanic, and ask about the following:
  - Make sure the latest manufacturer's recommended maintenance has been performed.
  - Your belts might need to be replaced and fluids replaced or topped off.
  - Adequate air pressure in the tires not only will help prevent tires from wearing out prematurely or blowing, but it also helps gas mileage. If you have a long drive, check the air pressure along the way and fill your tires as needed.
  - Get a roadside emergency kit that includes road flares, jumper cables, matches, a tire pressure gauge, and a first aid kit. If you'll be driving in cold weather, always pack extra blankets and drinking water.

- **Clean:** You'll probably want to seriously clean house before you move out, especially if you're renting and want to retain your apartment's deposit. You could do this yourself, arrange for a cleaning service to give the place a thorough scrubbing, or just let the property manager take the cleaning cost out of your deposit. If you've lived in your home a long time, a clutter cleaning home organization service can help you review your things and determine what to keep, give away, or toss. See Chapter 11 for more tips.

> MY EXPERIENCE
>
> *We tried to clean our apartment before moving out and cleaned the vast majority of the place, but there were some stubborn stains in the kitchen that we weren't able to clean up. Because the property manager had to call in someone to clean those, we didn't receive our deposit back even though it was mostly clean. My advice would be that if you're going to clean, clean it all; otherwise, have someone else do it.*

- **Gather personal documents:** Go to your doctors, dentists, lawyer, accountant, veterinarian, and schools to pick up x-rays, tax forms, transcripts, and other personal records so that you can take them with you.

- **Computer backup:** Back up your computer before you leave. You may already store email and photos online, but other documents could be burned to disc, saved on an external hard drive that you move separately, or uploaded to online storage.

- **Prepare appliances:** If you're bringing your refrigerator, washer, or other appliances, the manufacturer might have a recommended procedure before moving it, such as to defrost and drain your refrigerator. Check the owner's manuals.

- **Buy clothes:** If you'll be changing climates, look into essential weather-appropriate clothing before you get there. The same applies if you'll be moving to a more formal office culture and need some suits, ties, or dresses for your first week.

Turn off Services

- **Turn off utilities:** Turn off your utilities before you leave. Call ahead and indicate your last day so that things will be shut off. Write down or take a picture of the last reading on the meter as evidence in case your utility providers don't shut off your service promptly and extra charges appear on your bill later.

- **Turn off or change media services:** Depending on where you get your TV, Internet, phone service, and newspaper from, you might be able to change your service to your new address. However, if your new area is served by different companies, you will have to terminate your service. You might need to return your cable box or satellite dish, so make time to do this a few days before you move out.

- **Terminate other services:** Look through your credit card statement, or keep a copy of each bill to figure out what you'll need to cancel or change your address for, like a health club subscription or lawn service.

- **Forward mail:** Fill out a change of address notification with the Postal Service, which will forward your mail for the next year. This doesn't forward all your junk mail, but will forward magazines, credit card bills, and letters from your forgetful grandmother.

> ### MY EXPERIENCE
>
> *We've forwarded our mail every time we have moved and there's always been a random doctor bill, wedding invitation, or other notification that has been sent to our old address after the move. Forwarding our mail also seems like a nice courtesy so that the next person who takes our address doesn't get stuck with our mail.*

- **Bank or credit union:** If your bank or credit union doesn't have a branch in your new location, or if you will switch banks, it will be easier to close your account before you leave.

- **Take care of debts and warrants:** An outstanding debt or warrant can come back to bite you. Even if you're moving out of state, your warrant will appear the next time you have an encounter with law enforcement and could lead to you being detained by police for a minor traffic offense even if you are not extradited. Warrants could also impede your ability to get a job or secure a driver's license.

Change Addresses

Be sure to change your address on all your accounts as soon as you are able to receive mail at your new address. It may take a few weeks for magazines to start being sent to your new address. This could be a good time to set up paperless bank statements and automatic payment for your bills. Take note of all the service providers who will need your new address.

- **Doctor's offices:** Even if you'll be moving away, you don't want the person who moves in after you to know your name and your doctor. Accessing medical records or old medical bills are one way thieves steal someone's identity. Don't overlook your vet, dentist, and other specialists that you see infrequently.

- **Social Security Administration:** Periodic statements are sent in relation to your social security history.

- **Bank or credit union**

- **IRS**

- **Investments:** If you have money in any mutual funds, brokerages, IRA or 401(k) investments, trusts, annuities, or other financial vehicles, you will want to change your address with any financial institutions.

- **Personal advisors:** Your attorney, accountant, or stockbroker will need to know that you are moving. If your advisors aren't as familiar with the laws in your new area, they might be able to recommend someone else.

- **Loans:** Debts will eventually find you, so keeping the address correct will make sure that your financial information doesn't get into someone else's hands.

- **Credit and debit cards**

- **Charities**

- **Employer:** Even if you're quitting your job, your employer will need to send tax forms to your new address.

- **Magazine subscriptions**

- **Alma mater:** How will your college be able to write to you and ask for money if they don't have your address?

- **Online retailers:** Change your billing and mailing addresses ahead of time so that you don't order something and have it accidentally delivered to your old home after you move.

- **Online service providers:** Update your information anywhere you pay for movie streaming, gaming, or other online services.

- **Insurance providers:** Update insurance information for home, life, auto, rental, health, and any other insurance providers.

- **Mobile phone provider:** Check first to see whether your new area has good coverage by your existing provider. Most companies have maps showing their service levels. If your provider isn't available, look into switching companies before you move out. Otherwise, just changing your address should be all you need.

- **Pet ID:** If your pet has an ID chip implanted or your address on his or her collar, change the recorded address.

- **Family and friends:** Of course, people will need to know how to mail things to you.

WORKSHEET: ADDRESS CHANGE LOG

Write down all service providers who will need your new address and mark down the date when you notify each one.

Date Notified	Company	Phone Number or Website	Account No.
	e.g., "Total Rip-Off Cable"	1-800-555-4048	8150-4939-4

Other Preparation

- **Give notice to your landlord:** Leases usually require you to notify your landlord in writing at least two weeks and up to two months before moving out.

- **Give notice to your employer:** It's standard procedure to notify your boss that you will be leaving two weeks in advance. If you have a good relationship with your company and feel like notifying them further in advance, that would help them. But some companies terminate employees immediately after they give their notice, so do so at your own risk.

- **Resign from other obligations:** If you're a part of any boards or committees or have other volunteer obligations, give notice in advance so that you can be replaced.

Prepare for Your New Home

Some connections in your new area, like finding a doctor, can wait until you're settled but things like electricity service need to be set up before you arrive.

New residents establish an average of 71 new business relationships in their first few months in a new community (Nahajewski 2012). Here are some things to follow up on before you leave:

- **Confirm move-in details:** Call your landlord or realtor to schedule your move-in and any final paperwork that needs to be signed. You might need to reserve the apartment elevator in advance or check to see where the movers can park.

- **Confirm with the movers or truck rental:** Make sure that you are still scheduled on the date and time that you've recorded.

- **Take an inventory:** While your movers will take an inventory of your things, your own inventory can be used to confirm that they identified everything. An inventory will also be helpful to reference if you're looking for homeowner's insurance once you move.

- **Confirm hook-ups:** Before moving your appliances, make sure your new home has compatible hookups. That is, if you currently have a gas stove, make sure the new home has natural gas service. If you are planning to bring an electric clothes dryer, make sure your new home is wired for higher voltage service.

- **Set up utilities:** Will you be responsible for setting up your utilities? Many apartments will take care of all utilities for you, but find out for sure if you need to set up electricity, natural gas, water, or sewer service. Some markets have electricity provided by a single governmental entity. Other deregulated markets let you choose a specific provider. Find out from your realtor or the property manager the different service providers in your new area.

- **Set up media service:** Your new area might have other types of options for TV, Internet, and phone service. Maybe you used to use a satellite dish for TV, but your new condo doesn't allow them. Perhaps you're in a good position to receive TV via an over-the-air antenna. In more rural areas, DSL Internet service isn't available. In some more urban areas, you can use wireless broadband Internet or fiber optic Internet service.

- **Garbage collection:** You might need to schedule garbage collection at your new home and make sure you have the correct containers.

- **Security system:** If you want a home security system, you can buy direct or from a re-seller. Wireless security systems are coming into favor while some alarm providers may still use equipment that was created over a decade ago. Check on the fees; some charge more for carbon monoxide or fire monitoring. Get recommendations and check with the Better Business Bureau.

- **Parking permit:** Some neighborhoods have regulations for parking on the street. Check with the city's transportation or parking enforcement office to get a sticker for your car.

- **Insurance:** Your existing home insurance coverage might not apply or transfer to your new area, and you might need to purchase coverage for a new liability, such as flooding. If your health insurance ends before your new coverage begins, be sure to obtain temporary coverage to fill in the gap. The work and stress of moving can leave you more susceptible to illness or injury.

- **Enroll at new schools:** Most school districts or private schools will have a process identified on their website for enrolling. This will include identifying which school your child is assigned to based on where you live, the forms you have to fill out, and how to submit your information.

- **Contact people in your new city:** If you have family or professional relationships in the area, reach out to them to let them know you are coming and try to make a date to meet up.

- **Order things for your new home:** Once the previous tenant moves out, you might want to order things online and have them delivered to your new home if someone will be able to receive packages for you, such as at an apartment building. For example, if you will arrive before your movers do, have an air mattress delivered there and waiting for you.

- **Arrange for services to be done:** If you know that your new place needs pest extermination, a good lawn mowing, or a paint job, schedule those before your moving truck arrives. Your realtor might even be willing to let any service providers into the home if you're not there yet.

WORKSHEET: TO DO BEFORE YOU LEAVE

Make your own checklist of things that you want to do before you leave—either including or in addition to the details in the previous lists.

- ☐ _____
- ☐ _____
- ☐ _____
- ☐ _____
- ☐ _____
- ☐ _____
- ☐ _____
- ☐ _____
- ☐ _____
- ☐ _____
- ☐ _____
- ☐ _____
- ☐ _____
- ☐ _____
- ☐ _____
- ☐ _____
- ☐ _____
- ☐ _____
- ☐ _____
- ☐ _____
- ☐ _____
- ☐ _____
- ☐ _____
- ☐ _____

LETTING PEOPLE KNOW

At some point, you'll need to tell select people that you're moving. You could choose to do this as soon as you have the idea or wait until you have your job, home, and schools lined up.

> ## MY EXPERIENCE
>
> *When we were thinking of moving, we let our family and friends know that we were interested in the idea. However, they were surprised to find out how serious we were. As more plans solidified and the date approached, we gradually told more and more people. I stayed mum at work until I gave my notice. Some people were disappointed at the news and tried to discourage us while others were excited and supportive.*

Saying Goodbye

At some point you will want to say goodbye to people you care about, preferably in person. This could be done through a going-away party or some other social situation.

You may want to create moving announcements—for email, a card online, or an actual postcard. If you write personalized letters to everyone before you leave, include the new address and a picture of your new place.

While saying your goodbyes, spend time with people doing things that you enjoy. Try to enjoy the last moments before you leave. You may stay upbeat and positive; just remember that sharing emotions with others can be a positive bonding experience too. Consider the words of Dr. Seuss: "Don't cry because it's over. Smile because it happened."

If you maintain good relationships with friends, you can call them if you get lonely in your new place, keep up with news, and look forward to seeing them when you visit. With so many communication options, it's easier than ever to stay in touch with old friends, but it can be hard to stay connected as your lives separate over time.

If people want to give you something as a going-away gift, you could share a wish list of household gifts you will need in your next place, like cookware, linens, and decorations. Sentimental gifts like a photo college, ticket stubs of time spent together, or souvenirs from your current home could be special. Practical items can be helpful for your journey, like home-made snacks or a book to read.

• • •

As you get closer to the reality of relocating, your thoughts and feelings will probably change. The effort of choosing your place and housing will be replaced by the activity of actually moving. It won't be just a mental exercise anymore. Now that you'll be fully in action, you may be struck by the reality of the situation. While it's hard work to deal with the physical move, the emotional fatigue, the anxiety of uncertainty ahead, and the grief of saying goodbye, this can also be a stimulating time.

MOVING AND ARRIVING

11 Pack Up

There's so much to figure out in order to move. Fortunately, after finding a job, deciding where you're going to move to, and arranging the details of how you're going to move, most of the planning and deciding is out of the way. Now that you've laid the groundwork for a successful move, most of what's left involves physical work like actually packing and moving.

PLANNING TO PACK

To avoid running out of time before the movers arrive, pack as much as you can as soon as you can. Make a goal to pack a certain number of boxes per week.

> MY EXPERIENCE
>
> *Most of our things were packed at our home during the final week before moving. It was remarkable how few things we actually needed to get by for a week.*

Step-by-Step Plan

	STEP	HOW LONG TO START BEFORE MOVE	DURATION
THE MOVE			
	Prepare	**3–8 weeks**	**1–4 weeks**
1.	Acquire moving materials		
	Pack	**2–6 weeks**	**2–6 weeks**
2.	Out-of-season clothes and decorations	4–6 weeks	1–3 weeks
3.	Books, movies, games, and other media you don't plan to use	2–6 weeks	1–3 weeks
4.	Any other non-essential items	1–4 weeks	1–4 weeks
5.	Essentials to fit in your suitcase	1–2 weeks	1–2 weeks
6.	Daily use items (e.g., clothes, dishes)	1–2 weeks	1–2 weeks

PACKING

Supplies to Have on Hand

If you'll be packing everything yourself, be sure to have plenty of packing materials. You don't want to be scrambling for boxes, markers, or tape the day before your move, so buy more than you think you'll need.

Moving Boxes

Unless you're paying someone to pack everything for you, moving boxes are to a move as dishes are to dinner. So gather plenty of boxes—ideally, they're sturdy and consistently sized so that you can stack them.

It can be helpful if you've kept boxes from your last move or if you've kept any original packaging for odd-shaped or fragile items.

A wardrobe box can be especially helpful, as you can just transfer hanging clothes from the closet to the box, rather than have to fold them all.

Don't worry about having too many boxes, as you could give them to movers, leave them for someone else you know, or just recycle them. Here are some places to find boxes:

- Try family, friends, and co-workers who have recently moved.

- Check local apartment complexes for boxes left over from people who have recently moved in. Try contacting the apartment manager.

- Local grocery, book, and liquor stores, fast food restaurants, and other retail places receive a lot of boxes. Try checking in the back, asking a store employee, or peering inside their recycle bin.

- Self-storage and truck rental places have boxes for sale. Some truck rental facilities have a "take a box, leave a box" program with an area where you can take other people's used boxes.

- On Craigslist or Freecycle.org, try to find someone giving away or selling boxes in your area.

- Your employer may receive boxes for computers, printer paper, bathroom supplies, and other things. Ask your office manager or facilities person.

Tools to Move Things More Easily and Safely

- **Hand truck:** If you're moving things yourself, borrow, rent, or buy a dolly or hand truck with which to lift and move boxes and furniture much more easily. This is less helpful if stairs are involved but can save you lots of effort over flat, smooth surfaces. You could strain your back with all the lifting required during a move, so use one of these and use it smartly—don't overload it. To load it, have someone pull the top of the box away from the truck, lifting a bottom edge off the ground, then slide the hand truck underneath as far as possible. Tilt the hand truck back, and move it slowly so that your load doesn't shift.

- **Tools for furniture disassembly:** You might need a tool set including a screwdriver or hex key to take some furniture or large items apart to make them easier to move.

- **Heavy-duty garbage bags:** These are useful for carrying awkward-sized things, taking things to donate, and taking out the garbage before you go. Be aware that plastic bags may cause clothing to "sweat" due to temperature changes and the airtight nature of plastic bags.

- **Shoulder or forearm moving straps**: Use these straps to help you lift large pieces of furniture more easily without hurting your back. Back support belts are commonly used to protect against back injury, but there's limited evidence that they actually work.

- **Carpet sliders**: These discs, placed under furniture, make it easier to slide across a carpeted floor.

- **Floor mat**: A mat can provide extra traction to stop you from slipping if it's raining when you move or if you have slick areas to travel over.

Materials to Secure Things

- **Packing tape**: Use tape to securely close your boxes. Don't use tape on any delicate surfaces. While taping drawers closed can keep them from sliding open when furniture is being carried, it could also peel off any wood veneer, so it's better to use rope, twine, or stretch wrap.

- **Twine or rope**: If you'll be loading things in a moving truck yourself, use twine or rope to prevent things from moving around. Tie together pieces of your bed frame and use twine to keep drawers closed.

Materials to Protect Things

- **Packing bubbles**: Wrap delicate items with bubble wrap or put them inside boxes to keep things from moving. If you tend to order merchandise online, hang onto the packing materials that come with your orders.

- **Old newspapers or magazines**: Newsprint doesn't cushion things as well as air bubbles do and can also leave behind ink, but it's an adequate replacement for bubble wrap, cheaper, and usually easier to come by.

- **Packing peanuts**: This lightweight packaging and cushioning material can be used to protect your things. These are usually made from Styrofoam, but starch-based packing peanuts (made from food crops) are also available and are non-toxic and biodegradable.

- **Furniture pads**: These thick fabric pads can be wrapped around your furniture and large electronics to protect them from being damaged or from causing damage to walls and doorways. Most movers can provide these, but you can also use a couple layers of your own extra blankets, though blankets are not as thick or durable.

- **Heavy duty stretch wrap**: Wrap this around upholstery to protect against scratches and dirt.

Materials to Organize Things

- **Labels:** Use labels to number your boxes, identify the contents, and tell which room they go to. You could also apply labels to each end of electronics cords to tell you what they belong to.

- **Markers:** Plain old black will do, but color-coding can be helpful. You could write on the labels with a marker color that corresponds to the specific room it goes in. For example, use the orange marker for the kitchen or the blue one for the bathroom.

- **Plastic baggies:** If you have any furniture to disassemble or pictures to dismount from the wall, use a plastic baggie to organize any screws, washers, or other small things that need to be kept together. Write on the plastic baggie with a marker to indicate what the screws belong to, then tape the bag to a safe spot on the furniture where it won't be scraped off.

- **Pen and paper:** For writing down inventory, keeping notes on where you've packed things, or keeping track of any reminders for yourself.

Box Labeling

Labeling each box can help you unpack efficiently. Here are some things you could include:

- **Room:** Indicate where it goes so that the box gets put in the right room the first time. If you have multiple rooms of the same type (for example, bedrooms or bathrooms), it can be hard for your movers to know which room is which. In the new place, you could post a sign by the doorway of each room to help them. For quick identification, you could match a color and a unique symbol on the labels with a color and symbol that you post near the doorway. If you have children, letting them design the symbol that goes on their boxes could be fun.

- **Basic contents:** To help you know what's in each box, list a few things as you pack. That way, when you're desperately looking for toilet paper at your new home, you can find it easily (without having to open five boxes). Put thought into your labels—a box called "jewelry and rare coins" will be more appealing to dishonest movers than "junk from closet."

- **Unique number:** Movers often number each box and write an inventory, but your own number can help you track the boxes. Keep a list or spreadsheet that identifies each box, what's inside, and where it goes to help you find things more quickly when unpacking.

- **Priority:** It might take a while to unpack all your boxes after you arrive. Some boxes will be more important to unpack than others. Make a box or two of necessities and label them as the top priority to be unloaded and unpacked first. Include things like utensils and paper plates for the kitchen; towels and a shower curtain for the bathroom; and bed sheets, pillows, and a comforter for the bedroom.

- **Owner:** Another way of helping your family find their own boxes is to identify each box by its owner.

- **Fragile:** While labeling something as fragile when shipping it has been shown to increase the risk of breakage, your movers may be more careful with fragile items—hoping for a tip, or at the very least not wanting to have to reimburse you for breakage.

> MY EXPERIENCE
>
> *We labeled our boxes and kept track of the contents in a spreadsheet. A few of those boxes were never unpacked, including high school yearbooks, old electronics, and other mementos. The labeling has been helpful when I've had to dig through the closet for something specific, like Christmas decorations.*

Items to Keep with You

When you're packing, you might not want to put everything in the moving van. When all your worldly possessions are somewhere on a truck between Walla Walla and Waxahachie, there are some things to keep on your person to minimize the risk of loss:

- **Travel items:** Depending on how long the trip will be, you'll probably want to pack as if you're going on vacation. Keep a few changes of clothes, your toiletries, basic first aid supplies, and other personal items. *Set these items aside early*, possibly in a bag or suitcase so that you don't accidentally pack them.

- **Identification documents:** Your driver's license or state ID, passport, birth certificate, and social security card are some of the most important official documents you own. Keep them with you or in your luggage.

- **Money:** Make sure you have enough cash for the journey and to tip the movers. Bring along a credit card and bank card as well.

- **Move-related documents:** Key documents of information on your new home, like a lease or printed directions, should probably go with you. Same goes for a job offer.

- **Legal, contractual, and financial records:** Carrying a file cabinet with you could be difficult, but if there are important original documents you own, like the deed to your home, investment holdings, or documents with your social security number, make sure those are being transported safely.

- **Photos and other mementos:** You might not want to take all of your photo albums with you, but you may well own some priceless keepsakes. Be sure to back up your digital photos.

- **Snacks:** Having some healthy snack food with you can be convenient for the journey, especially when traveling with children.

- **Important items for children:** Your kids will feel more comfortable if they have a favorite toy, stuffed animal, or book to bring along with them during the adventure.

- **Household items you'll need:** While you will be buying a lot once you arrive, you might want to bring some basic things with you so that you don't have to run too many errands right after arriving. This list could include toilet paper, paper towels, soap, a flashlight, and disposable cups and bowls.

- **Anything else you'll need while your things are in boxes:** If your movers won't arrive at your new home until after you do, consider what you'll need for the first day of work or school.

Pet Materials

If you're moving with an animal, there are many more things you'll want to keep on hand. Be sure that their crate is well ventilated and has a leak-proof bottom with layers of absorbent lining. Place a toy in the carrier and a blanket inside and let your pet get used to it before the move.

- Carrier or crate

- Blanket to cover crate

- Crate water bottle

- Extra water

- Mattress or bed

- Bags for their waste

- Food

- Favorite treat (especially for cats who are finicky about eating)

- Catnip

- Toys

- Medications

- Copy of records from the vet

- Leash and collar or harness

- New identification tags with new address

- Towels and disinfecting wipes for accidents

- Somewhere for your pet to urinate, such as a Doggie Pee Pad

- Sedatives (for your pet, not for you)

- Photos of your pet, including one for you and one for your carrier in case your pet gets separated from you or the carrier

Packing and Moving Tips

As you start to pack your things and get ready for the day of the move, here are some general tips:

Take Care of Yourself

- **Eat healthy food:** Don't skip meals if you can help it. Keep your meals light and eat more complex carbohydrates (like beans, vegetables, and grain products); resist sugary or fatty snack foods like soda and chips. Avoid alcohol before doing any lifting, and save the beer for later as your reward for hard work.

- **Get plenty of sleep:** As busy as you may be, if you miss out on sleep, you're more likely to make mistakes or catch a cold and therefore be even more miserable during your move.

- **Set aside time to rest:** While you are busy and have a lot to do, try to make some time to relax when you're not packing. Have coffee with a friend, sit down and read a book, or watch a favorite movie to stay off your feet and give your body a chance to rest.

Packing Tips

- **Distribute heavy loads:** It may be tempting to put your entire rock collection in one box, but please look out for the health of whoever has to carry that box and distribute heavy items.

- **Clean and dust as you pack:** If you can, take a moment as you pack things to dust them or wipe them off. Hand wash outdoor equipment so that dirt and grime don't scratch or rub off on other things.

- **Cushion fragile items:** Packing your plates, glassware, and other fragile items does require some care to make sure that each item is protected and secure. Wrapping items with bubble wrap works, but newspaper, socks, and towels can also provide cushioning. Pieces of cardboard are helpful for separating and protecting fragile items.

- **Pack things tightly:** Even if fragile items don't touch when you pack them, items can shift in a box during a 1,000 mile journey. You'll want to pack the box full so that contents are snug and don't move around when the box is being moved. When loading a truck, keep everything tied town with twine and put blankets, towels, or furniture pads in between hard objects so that they don't wear on each other.

- **Pack what you can:** While movers will wrap up most furniture and awkward sized items, like brooms and tall lamps, you'll probably want to pack as much as you can in boxes. This way, you can make sure that things are packed securely. If you're paying movers by the hour, your packing will also save you money.

- **Wrap chair legs and furniture edges:** If you're doing the moving by yourself, take special note of vulnerable parts of furniture (like chair legs and table edges) and protect them with corrugated cardboard or furniture pads.

- **Use wardrobe boxes wisely:** Wardrobe boxes are intended for hanging clothes. However, you can fit things in at the bottom or put other awkwardly sized things in with your clothes.

- **Pack and stack carefully:** Pack your boxes with the weight evenly distributed and stack lighter boxes on top of heavy ones.

Logistics

- **Turn off your fridge:** If you'll be moving or storing your freezer and refrigerator, turn them off two days before moving so that water can be drained out.

- **Take photos:** Take pictures of valuables as they are being packed in case anything is damaged by the movers.

Lifting and Moving

Lifting and moving heavy things during a move is a common cause of injury. Here are some pointers to protect yourself:

- **Don't lift if you don't have to:** Use a dolly or hand truck to help you move things around. Rather than strain yourself, partner with other lifters. Try to set each box down in a good location so that you don't have to move it again.

- **Plan your path:** Before you lift something, first make sure the path is clear and know where you're going to put it.

- **Test first:** Push a heavy item you're about to move to assess how heavy it is.

- **Use good technique:** Get as close to the load as you can before you lift it, and then keep the load close to you. Bend at your knees and try to keep your back straight and vertical so that your legs do the work. Avoid twisting, especially when holding heavy objects.

- **Move carefully:** Use slow and smooth movements.

- **Don't overdo it:** While it might be tempting to carry as much as possible to reduce the number of trips back and forth, pace yourself. Don't overdo it. If you feel yourself having to strain to lift something, stop and get help.

Cleaning

You might want to clean your place before you move out, either to receive your initial deposit back or save money on cleaners.

Things to Consider

- **What's required?:** If you're renting, find out what needs to be cleaned when you leave. Some apartment managers will shampoo or possibly replace the carpet. You may need to repaint the walls or just apply primer. It's possible to let management handle the cleaning and take that fee out of your deposit.

- **Ventilate:** If you use cleaners that produce fumes, keep windows open and run any fans to keep fresh air circulating.

- **Start at the back:** Begin cleaning in the room farthest from the front door and close rooms as you work towards the entrance.

- **Get help and make it fun:** Recruit family or friends to help clean. Make it more fun by listening to music while you work or going out for dinner when you're done.

- **Think tall:** If you're short like me, don't forget high surfaces like the top of the fridge or the tops of cabinet doors.

Kitchen

- **Clean the fridge:** Remove any food. Then remove all shelves and drawers from the refrigerator and hand-wash them. Wipe down the interior of the fridge and freezer.

- **Clean the oven:** Some ovens have a self-clean function to burn off residue. Alternatively, you can use store-bought oven cleaners, though they often have corrosive chemicals, or you can create an oven-cleaning paste with baking soda and vinegar.

- **Wipe down surfaces:** Wipe down other surfaces like cabinets, light fixtures, countertops, the dishwasher, and the microwave.

- **Clean behind appliances:** To do a really good job, pull out the stove and refrigerator (while taking care not to scratch the floor) and clean the part of the floor that isn't usually seen. You might possibly find something you'd lost back there in addition to the dirt, bugs, food, and stains.

Floors, Windows, and Fixtures

- **Clean floors:** Treat any spots on carpet; you could borrow a steam cleaner to clean more deeply. Vacuum your carpet and mop your hard floors.

- **Clean windows:** Wipe off dirt from the windows and wash or at least dust the blinds (you'll be amazed at how dirty they are).

- **Wipe things that accumulate dust:** Wipe off the blades of the ceiling fans and light fixtures.

- **Clean sinks:** Use a toothbrush and special cleanser to remove water spots.

- **Remove dirt from walls:** Wash the walls with water and vinegar and use a product like a Magic Eraser® to remove marks or stains.

When you move out of a rental, try to be present for the final inspection so that you can address any concerns at that time. If you can't be there, take pictures of your apartment for your records in case the manager says you damaged the place. Also, make sure that your landlord has your new address in order to send back your security deposit. Hang on to your lease or rental agreement and other records in case there are problems later.

. . .

With your things packed and your old place cleaned, there's not much left to do but be on your way to your new home.

12 Move

All the preparation you've done has led you to moving day. It can be taxing, but if you've made it this far, you can handle whatever the day brings you. Start out with a deep breath and a sense of anticipation for the journey ahead.

ADVICE FOR MOVING DAY

There are a variety of tips to be aware of as your boxes are being carried off.

If you have young children, this is a great time for friends or relatives to take the kids out for a special day together. Or you could hire a babysitter or let the kids have fun with boxes and bubble wrap. Older children might be able to help move.

Keep a box unsealed for any final things that turn up. Set aside critical things you need to bring with you, like keys and documents, in a safe place where they will not be touched during the commotion of moving day. (We used the empty refrigerator.) This way, they're less likely to disappear on their own.

Make sure to double-check every corner of your home before you leave to confirm that nothing is left behind.

Advice for Doing the Move Yourself

If you're doing the work yourself, start the day early and dress appropriately with sturdy shoes and clothing that isn't too loose.

If friends are coming to help, think ahead so that you can delegate and give them instructions on packing and labeling, moving boxes, dusting, and wrapping furniture.

Advice When Renting a Moving Truck

When you go to pick up the truck, make sure that whoever will drive it (if not yourself) is present with their driver's license. Typically, the rental company won't allow unauthorized people to drive it. Be aware that rental truck companies have a minimum age of 24 for a driver.

Before you drive, adjust your mirrors carefully. You'll have to rely on those side mirrors, so get a sense of where your blind spots are. When backing up, have someone guide you and keep him or her in your line of sight. It may take a while to get used to the vehicle's size and weight, and you'll need to remember to brake earlier and allow a wider area for turns. Know your truck's height so that you don't scrape the roof in a parking garage. Drive slowly and follow any speed limits for trucks. Use the parking brake when you park.

For safety, put the heaviest stuff in the middle of the truck. Also, each time you park the truck, walk around to inspect the tires and periodically inspect the lights and door locks. You might need to use a padlock on the rear door.

Advice When Using Movers

The mover will inventory the items to be moved and will provide what is called a *Bill of Lading*, which is a contract to have the movers transport your things. Read through both documents. Be sure you understand them and confirm that they are accurate before signing anything.

Any successful move involves a cooperative relationship between you and your movers. Treat the movers with respect. Offer any food or drinks you still have to the movers. They may not accept, but they'll be appreciative. Stick around to assist, answer questions, and to supervise the operation.

It is customary to tip your movers—especially if their professionalism, effort, and efficiency exceeded your expectations. A reasonable range to start with would be $10 to $30. You can adjust upward—if service was exceptional or the move was difficult due to stairs or awkward items—or downward, if the movers were late, disorganized, or unprofessional. If you have any issues or concerns, try to remain calm and discuss with the lead mover, who is usually also the driver.

Pet Tips

Some pets may be extremely uncomfortable with all the action. They will benefit by being entertained outside, in a separate room, or by being contained in their carrier. To help keep your pet comfortable, maintain the usual feeding schedule.

Consider boarding your pet for a couple days during the hectic times of moving. Your pet might be less stressed by being boarded than by staying amid all the activity at home. You might also board your pet while you unpack at the new home and settle in.

If you do keep your pet in the house on moving day and don't want to close them off in a specific room, dog and cat repellent spray can be effective at creating boundaries. Some sprays are acceptable for indoor and outdoor use and could keep pets out of an area, off the stairs, or away from boxes with fragile items.

Cats shed more when stressed and may need more grooming time.

Flying with a Pet

Moving a pet by air is potentially dangerous. If your pet will be traveling in cargo, write the words "FRAGILE, LIVE ANIMAL" and "THIS SIDE UP" clearly on the outside of their container.

Feed your pet a light meal five to six hours before flight time. Do not give it water less than two hours before takeoff, except on very hot days.

Take your pet for a walk at the airport and give any necessary medications. Make sure your dog takes care of its business before the flight. Most airlines have pet relief areas outside of security, though a few have relief areas inside security.

Close your pet carrier securely and fasten your pet's leash to the outside of the container. Your pet must be kept in the carrier at all times, except when going through airport security. Even if you don't normally use a leash with your pet, fasten the leash during the security screening, just in case.

You'll need essential paperwork handy, including a recent health certificate and special boarding pass. Put an extra copy in your pet's carrier as well.

Driving with a Pet

Make sure you'll have treats, food, water, and bathroom material for all your pets. Spoil your pet as much as possible, spending plenty of time with them and easing their stress. Don't overfeed your pet, though, as that could contribute to motion sickness. Offer their favorite treats to encourage them to eat. A sedated animal may not drink as much; keep an eye on their water intake so that they stay hydrated. Keep a time log of any sedatives you administer to prevent an accidental overdose.

You may have found lodging that accepts pets, but do everything you can to prevent your pets from soiling the carpet or damaging the furniture, as the hotel can charge you for this. You might keep your pet in the crate most of the time. If not, be sure to put the "do not disturb" sign on the door so that housekeeping doesn't open the door and let your pet escape. Some dogs get lonely, so don't leave them alone if they'll bark and annoy other guests. If any hotel staff are especially accommodating to you and your pet, it's appropriate to tip them.

While on the road, you'll need to be attentive to the position of the sun and make sure that the temperature is just right, especially for small animals like hamsters and gerbils. If you have to leave your pet in the car in warm weather, lock the doors and open the windows for ventilation. When the car is off, the cabin can become quite cold or hot quickly, depending on outside temperatures.

Try to maintain a regular schedule for your pet's feeding, recreation, and bathroom stops.

If you put a bowl of water in your pet's crate, the car's movement will cause much of it to slosh out, so be sure to make plenty of stops for water and exercise for cats and dogs. One option to keep your pet more comfortable is to bring a supply of water from home—your pet is used to the taste.

Pets can get motion sickness just like people, so watch for that and make sure your pet has plenty of air. If you've moving a bird, you might leave its cage covered to keep it calm.

AFTER YOUR THINGS ARE GONE

Once your things have been loaded into a truck and you're about to leave your old place for good, the reality of the situation may hit you and be a little overwhelming.

You may want to stop and reflect a bit before leaving. Remembering all the experiences and good times you had at this place you've called home can be emotional.

> MY EXPERIENCE
>
> *When we left our apartment in Texas, after the movers had left, my wife and I were alone in an empty apartment. We had planned to leave the next morning, so the day the movers came seemed anticlimactic and we just had to keep ourselves busy until we could leave.*
>
> *While we weren't very emotionally attached to that home, our next move was after living in Seattle for three years. That was where we made so many memories discovering Seattle together. Even though we were just moving a mile away when we left that place, I broke down and cried. I was so sad to be leaving such a special place.*

You might do a final walk-through to make sure that the movers didn't leave anything behind. Also, make sure all windows are closed and locked, the hot water is turned off, and the thermostat has been adjusted.

WHILE ON YOUR WAY

Being "en route" during a move is an interesting time because you don't really have a home. Your ID card and all your documents may not have been changed yet; you're neither here nor there. You're a vagabond, roaming the country just as our pioneers did, in search of a better life.

Eating

It's hard to eat well during a move. But it's worth it to give a little thought and preparation to getting a balanced diet.

Fast food is plentiful and can be appealing when you're on the road or in an airport. But there are other alternatives.

If you're driving, bring a cooler. Stop by the grocery store or farmers market before you leave and grab some fruits that travel well, like apples, bananas, oranges, grapes, and blueberries, and vegetables like carrots, celery, and bell peppers.

Additionally, nuts and trail mixes are good snacks and good sources of protein. Granola bars, single-serving boxes of cereal, small yogurts, and string cheese can be good options. If you'll be traveling for a few days, you could even buy a loaf of bread and peanut butter.

Regardless of how you're traveling, it's important to stay hydrated. Buy some bottled water to have with you and refill them as needed.

Safety

If you're driving and stopping at motels, park in a well-lit parking spot. You could request a room from which you can see your vehicle. In unfamiliar areas, you might want to use a steering wheel lock and car alarm.

> MY EXPERIENCE
>
> *When we moved, the car trunk and back seat were full of things that we didn't have the movers take. We had things like our external hard drive, blankets we needed for the nights without our bed, as well as extra clothes, makeup that we thought could melt if left with the movers, and various other things. We realized that leaving the backseat full of things could make our car a target for theft. So, at every hotel we stayed at on the five nights of our journey, we emptied the back seat and brought things into our hotel room.*

• • •

However you're moving—by plane, train, or automobile—try to enjoy it. Congratulate yourself on the fact that you've already accomplished a lot. It takes ambition to move, and you have taken great initiative. Everything ahead will be an adventure!

13 Arrive and Move In

It can be very exciting when you first arrive at your new home. Take a deep breath and celebrate your success.

Now, let's see how you can move in smoothly, anticipate expenses, and have an exciting year.

PLANNING TO MOVE IN

Step-by-Step Plan

	STEP	HOW LONG TO START BEFORE MOVE	DURATION
ARRIVE AND MOVE IN			
	Move In		
1.	Unpack and put things away	Immediately	1–8 weeks
	Making Your Home		
2.	Decorate and purchase housewares	Immediately	1–4 weeks
3.	Prepare for safety	Immediately	1 week

Budgeting

Let's anticipate the expenses you might incur in replacing any household items you left behind and decorating your new place to make it your own. It's a fact that people spend two to three times more on furnishings, appliances, and home repairs in their first year in a new area than in any other year (Siniavskaia 2008).

Low budget estimate: $385
If you don't cook or are bringing food with you, your first grocery bill should be low. You'll also save money if you don't own a car.

Mid budget estimate: $1,550
Decorations can add up quickly. You might have a couple rooms to decorate and want to buy some curtains or a couple inexpensive wall decorations.

High budget estimate: $10,400
Making a home feel like your own could require not only window dressings but repainting the walls, adding art, and even replacing the fixtures and buying new furniture that fits and coordinates.

Example Expenses

EXPENSE	LOW ESTIMATE (DOLLARS)	MEDIUM ESTIMATE (DOLLARS)	HIGH ESTIMATE (DOLLARS)
ARRIVAL			
Cleaning supplies	40	60	100
Restock fridge and pantry	100	300	1,000
MOVE IN			
Tip for movers	0	20	60
Decorations and household purchases	200	1,000	7,000
Home repairs (if owning)	20	100	2,000
IF MOVING TO A NEW STATE			
Vehicle registration	20	50	200
State identification card	5	20	40
TOTAL	**385**	**1,550**	**10,400**

WHEN YOU ARRIVE

First Tasks

Arriving at the new place brings a variety of emotions: excitement to be in your new home, relief that you made it, and satisfaction (and pride!) that you were able to make it happen.

You'll probably need to run to the grocery store for paper towels, cleaning products, soap, paper plates and cups, and some food. Stock your fridge so that you'll have things to eat and drink while you're moving in and unpacking. You might need to replace things like condiments, sauces, and cereals.

If you arrive before your possessions do, use the time to figure out where the movers should place each piece of furniture. Draw a floor plan for each room, sketch in where furniture goes, and post it on the room's doorsill.

You may want to take pictures or a video of the place before things are moved in. You could send a postcard or publish photos online so that people know you've arrived.

MY EXPERIENCE

Once we saw the city skyline emerge just ahead on the highway, we were so excited to be arriving in Seattle and amazed at how far we'd come. Arriving at our new home on a beautifully clear day in February was a magical experience that made all our efforts worthwhile.

We knew that we would arrive in Seattle before our moving company and had planned to spend a week sleeping on the floor at our new home. It wasn't the most comfortable sleep, but with a few blankets, it was cheaper than other options. It felt odd that we had so few things to fill the unit, but we picked up some essentials at the nearby grocery store and made it through the week.

When Entering a Rental Unit

You should do a thorough inspection as soon as you can. The property management company will often do the walkthrough with you and fill in a move-in damage report. Take this process seriously and look for any problems, such as scuffs on the walls, toilets that leak, or broken window screens, and make sure any problems are indicated on the report. You don't want to lose your deposit because you didn't spend the time to look carefully during that initial inspection.

Make sure that your utilities are turned on and that everything works. If you don't have hot water, call maintenance for help.

MOVING IN

When your things arrive, you'll have a ton of work to do, but each item that you unpack brings you one step closer to making this new place yours.

Movers

If you're using movers, confirm when they are scheduled to arrive and be there at that time. They may not give you a heads-up before they arrive, so plan to be home at the ready all day.

After they unload your things, check that all of your possessions have arrived—safely and without damage—before signing off on the moving job.

If things are missing or damaged, let the mover know. They will likely have you fill out a company claim form that you can submit. If you have to mail the claim form, it's recommended that you send it by certified mail and keep a copy for yourself.

Most respectable movers will attempt to settle the situation fairly and some movers will offer a discount on the spot to avoid a claim against them.

When it comes to signing the bill for your move, the fees should be what you expected based on your moving paperwork and the mover's published tariff. *If any of your possessions are damaged or lost, indicate this on the original copy of the inventory sheet before signing it.*

If you've been overcharged and the mover is not able to address your issue, contact the Surface Transportation Board at 1-866-254-1792. If issues are unresolved by the mover, you can contact the Federal Motor Carrier Safety Administration at nccdb.fmcsa.dot.gov. While they don't have the authority to resolve claims against the mover, they can initiate a federal investigation against the mover.

The Federal Trade Commission (FTC) Bureau of Consumer Protection is another path for submitting a complaint at www.ftc.gov/about-ftc/bureaus-offices/bureau-consumer-protection. The National Association of Attorneys General at www.naag.org links to the Attorney General in your old state and your new state. They can receive complaints against movers or direct you to the state agency that will receive a complaint.

If all else fails in resolving your situations with the mover, you can take legal action.

Moving Truck

If you've rented a moving truck, you'll probably want to fill it up with gas or be faced with the rental company's gas refueling fee. Your best bet is to return the vehicle during business hours and have an employee inspect the truck with you. This way, you can make sure that you're not incorrectly charged for any damage.

Unpacking

Your move isn't really complete until you've unpacked.

Some people may be inclined to take their time while others will finish unpacking as quickly as possible. Put things away in the order that works best for you. You could start by placing a few symbolic things, like photos, so that it starts to feel like home. Emptying wardrobe boxes into closets might help you feel that you are making good progress.

If you're moving with family members, you can coordinate your efforts. Have each person focus on unpacking things in a different area, or make teams: maybe one person can unpack kitchen boxes while the other person can put them away. Also, taping labels on kitchen drawers or cupboard doors can help everyone get oriented to where things are. You may want to set up your children's rooms first. Let them open the boxes that carry their toys and it will feel to them like their birthday all over again.

You could arrange things similarly to how they were in the old home or use this as an opportunity to try something new.

Your pets will be more comfortable if your furniture is in place before they get there. While you are busy moving boxes or unpacking, you could keep pets in a closed room with their toys so they are more comfortable.

To help you get through things quickly, try to make an immediate decision on where something should go. If you can't decide right away, put it down and move on to the next item. After you've handled the easy decisions, you can come back to some of the harder stuff more prepared to decide.

You may want to set all your boxes in the middle of the room to provide some extra motivation to unpack. An alternative strategy that allows for a slower pace is to set unpacked boxes in one corner of the room so that they are least in the way of using the space. In either case, keep walkways and hallways clear.

If you wait too long to unpack, your sealed boxes will just sit unopened in the closet. If you decide that you no longer need your collection of mix-tapes from high school after all, then go ahead and toss them now.

Don't overdo things. Leave some room on your couch to sit and rest when you need to. Feel free to schedule a massage after your move in to help relieve some stress.

MAKING YOUR HOME

Safety

There are a few simple steps you can take to make sure your home is safe.

Batteries in smoke detectors and carbon monoxide detectors need to be replaced periodically. Often, apartment management takes responsibility for replacing them, but ask. Also, check each room for a smoke detector and purchase a carbon monoxide detector if you don't have one. Find out where fire extinguishers are located within or outside of your building. Make sure that you have your own and know how to use it. A first aid kit is another must-have; check the Red Cross for a list of recommended items.

In case of fire or emergency, identify your evacuation route. If you're in a single-family home, this might be as easy as finding the nearest door. In a large apartment building, it could mean counting the doorways between yours and the fire exit, and knowing if there's an assembly area.

If you own your home or your lease allows it, you might want to buy new locks since you don't know who has copies of the key. Secure any external sliding glass doors with a locking bar and include locks on fence gates.

Also, be sure to set up any pet-proofing you had at your old home. Make sure your new yard is dog or cat proof, meaning that there is nothing dangerous in the yard and that your dog can't escape. You may want to keep outdoor cats inside a few days until they adjust.

Some people use automatic light timers or motion sensors to ensure adequate outside lighting.

If you're living on a managed property, look into your options for package deliveries; ask if your building's doorman can accept deliveries for you. Or, look for a mailbox service or post office box so that packages won't be left on your doorstep where anyone could take them (or where they could signal that you're not home).

Decorations and Household Purchases

You will likely want to make some improvements, whether it be landscaping or just hanging some new decorations inside. These costs add up, so set a budget that you can afford. You might want to attend to these tasks gradually later on, after most of the hard work of moving in is behind you. If you own your home and are considering some dramatic renovations, wait until you've lived there for a year to better understand what you want to do with the space.

Figuring out how to decorate a new home can be exciting or overwhelming.

If you're not sure what you want to do, an interior designer can help. If you have difficulty organizing your things, you could look into hiring a professional organizer through the National Association of Professional Organizers.

Painting is one of the most cost-effective ways to change the feel of a place. Replace the wallpaper, repaint a room, or just paint an accent wall in the living room to make the place your own. Some apartments offer repainting as a standard option; others will usually let you apply paint if it's not too dark.

You can buy new bedding to go with the new floor or buy pillows for your couch that coordinate with the walls. Adding curtains or drapes can improve the look of a room, keep out unwanted sunlight, and insulate drafty windows. And, though a little more costly, replacing light fixtures is another way to make a home feel like yours. You could even replace doorknobs, light switch covers, or other items in the home.

● ● ●

Moving into your new home marks a huge milestone. After all the work, you can start to settle in and discover what's around you.

14 Settle In and Look Ahead

The first year in a new place can be a very tumultuous time. If you're moving by choice, you might have a lot of fun discovering a whole new culture. If this is an unwanted move for you, you can still enjoy some of the adventure of finding people and places that you like.

A number of things could make for a rocky adjustment to your new town. For most of us, a smooth transition into a new living environment is a result of planning, a positive mindset, and some luck. Have the best first year you can—enjoying the excitement of your new home in discovering new things and meeting new people, adjusting well to the changes in your identity, and staying in contact with friends and family.

SETTLING IN

Now you can focus on acclimating yourself to a new area, new people, and establishing the kind of lifestyle you want.

Logistics for New Home

There are lots of things to figure out! Simple things like buying groceries may take some planning or exploration before you know which store to go to and how to get there. The new setting means that even going out for a simple meal can feel like an adventure.

> ### My Experience
>
> *While we knew how to get to work when we first arrived, our first trip to the grocery store was a bit of an adventure. Living in an area with good public transit, we decided to take the bus there, but we weren't used to having to carry our bags with us, so we bought more than we could carry comfortably. It took a while of trying different modes of transportation and different grocery stores before we found the right routine for us.*

If you are acquainted with anyone locally, you may want to meet with them when you first arrive to help you feel more comfortable and to get some tips.

Before starting your new job, take time to scout out the area for the shortest route to the freeway or local transit stops. If you have time before your start date, drive your commute one day just to see what it takes to get through traffic and arrive on time. Make sure your children know how to get to and from their schools, and rehearse the route with them. Once you meet your coworkers, you can ask around for traffic shortcuts or look into alternative transportation; maybe there's a carpool group or a bus that takes just as long but is less of a burden.

Chapter 10 had a list of things that you could set up in your new home. If you didn't do all of those before you moved, now is the time to do them. Here are some additional things to address:

- **Identification card:** If you have moved to a new state, you may be legally required to get a new state identification card. Your new state may even require that you retake your driving test. Look into when the state requires you to have this card and what you need to provide for proof of residence.

- **Car registration and license plates**: New license plates might be required for your car after living in a new state for 30 days. You will also likely need to pay a state registration fee.

- **Register to vote**: You will need to register to vote, often a few weeks before the next election. You can get the application online here: www.eac.gov/voter_resources/register_to_vote.aspx

- **Additional cards**: You may want to get a library card or a card for riding transit.

- **Pet licensing**: Get a new license for your pet through the city, if applicable. You might need a proof-of-vaccination form or information from your vet.

- **Safety information**: Save the non-emergency police number and other important phone numbers.

- **Bank or credit union**: Even if you can use the same bank in your new area, you might still want to set up a new account. Your bank account has to abide by the regulations in the state where you lived at the time it was set up. In some cases, laws in your new state may have advantages for you. For example, you might currently be paying a service fee or tax (in the old state) that would not be required if you created a new account. Setting up a new account means that you will have to update any direct deposit or automatic withdrawals you have set up. If you do have to set up an account with a new bank, look for features that are important to you, like ATM availability, low fees, and other services.

- **New doctors**: You'll need to find new health care providers including a general practitioner, dentist, and any specialists like dermatologists or gynecologists. Check to see where your health insurance is accepted and ask coworkers for referrals. As you look for doctors, consider their office hours, typical wait times to see the doctor, and any special medical needs you have.

- **Pharmacy**: Find the pharmacy that best suits your needs and bring in your standing prescriptions.

- **Find service providers**: You'll have to find new service providers to cut your hair, paint your nails, and clean your house. Online resources like Yelp can be great for this, or you can ask people you meet for recommendations. There are some companies like Our Town America from which you can request mailings with coupons and advertisements for local merchants.

Starting Good Habits

Just as you will have to start new routines for going to work and running errands, you also have the opportunity to start new habits. Immediately after relocating, you will be *more open to new experiences* than at any other time, excluding a major life change like getting married or having a baby. Moving disrupts your routines and puts you in a change-oriented mindset. In fact, you're more likely to follow through on resolutions right after a move than you are on New Year's Day.

You'll probably benefit from coming up with some goals for your next six months. Try to be realistic—running a marathon would be a stretch if you've never jogged a mile. Maybe you want to lose 15 pounds and start waking up early to go to the gym. It might be time to start volunteer work, stop over-committing, or switch to a vegetarian diet. This transition is a great time to make changes so you can start living the lifestyle you want.

Use the Worksheet: Goals and Habits to put your goals into words. If you write these down and put them where you'll see them regularly, you'll be more likely to follow through. Even if you aren't successful at all of your goals, don't discount any minor progress you are able to make—celebrate it!

WORKSHEET: GOALS AND HABITS

Goal/Habit 1: _____

Goal/Habit 2: _____

Goal/Habit 3: _____

Goal/Habit 4: _____

Goal/Habit 5: _____

Goal/Habit 6: _____

Goal/Habit 7: _____

Goal/Habit 8: _____

Goal/Habit 9: _____

Goal/Habit 10: _____

TAX DEDUCTIONS

There are a couple of little-known U.S. tax benefits to take advantage of when you move *for a new job*. While this doesn't make up for all of your costs, it does mean that you don't have to pay as much tax, as long as you have kept careful track of your expenses. There are rules and exceptions and a lot of fine print, but it's a good idea to tackle this as soon as you move in so that you don't forget or lose your receipts. Consult a tax professional if you have questions.

Moving Expenses

To deduct moving expenses, you have to be starting a new job shortly after moving and your new job has to be more than 50 miles from your previous residence.

If you used to live and work overseas and are now permanently retired, you can deduct moving expenses to the United States. Or if you lived overseas with a spouse, dependent, or someone you were a dependent of, you can deduct moving expenses if that person has died and you move back to the United States within six months of the death. Active-duty members of the Armed Forces are eligible if you are moving to or from a post of duty.

You can deduct expenses related to moving your stuff and moving yourself. Of course, there are many rules about what is allowable.

You can't deduct the cost of any meals. You also cannot deduct costs for sightseeing or traveling off of the "shortest, most direct route available by conventional transportation." If you choose to take the long way, you can still deduct what it would have cost you to take the shorter, quicker route. And if you and an immediate member of your household move separately, you can deduct the cost for each of you to move.

You can deduct expenses for your car, either at a set rate per mile or based on your actual costs for gasoline and oil changes, plus any tolls or parking fees.

The costs for moving your stuff, including "packing, crating, and transporting your household goods and personal effects and those of the members of your household" can be deducted, as can expenses of putting your things in storage for a period of time after you move out.

You can also deduct any costs of disconnecting utilities at your old home and connecting utilities at your new one.

There are a number of other rules and restrictions, and since taxes are involved, it can get complicated. Refer to IRS Publication 521 (www.irs.gov/uac/Publication-521,-Moving-Expenses) for all the details and use IRS form 3903 to list your expenses.

Job Search Expenses

You can deduct job search expenses if you're looking for a job *in the same field* as where you worked most recently and choose to itemize your deductions rather than taking the standard deduction. New graduates or people changing careers aren't eligible, neither are people who haven't worked in a significant period of time.

Only expenses above 2% of your adjusted gross income are deductible. For example, if your adjusted gross income is $50,000, then 2% of that is $1,000. If you have job search expenses of $1,500, then you can deduct $500 from your income.

Job search expenses are claimed as a miscellaneous itemized deduction. Allowed deductions include travel and transportation for job applications and interviews, lodging while traveling, expenses to improve your education or skills, professional résumé editing, and work clothes. Meal costs related to job searching can be deducted, whereas meal costs related to moving cannot.

Refer to IRS Publication 529 on miscellaneous deductions for more information: www.irs.gov/uac/Publication-529,-Miscellaneous-Deductions.

Other Financial Actions

After moving to a new city, revisit your financial health. Most moves involve a change in your regular expenses as well as your income, so make sure you have enough money on hand. You might revisit your estate plans and look into any applicable tax benefits.

DISCOVERING THINGS AND MEETING PEOPLE

The first two months in a new place are often the busiest as you set up your home and establish a new life. This time can be chaotic as you finish settling into your new home, figure out the best route to work, and watch for a good local hangout.

Every day, you'll see new people, places, and things. It's exciting to take advantage of the things that drew you to the town, whether sandy beaches, a vibrant neighborhood, or having family nearby. And by staying busy, you're less likely to become homesick.

Discovering the Town

Take time and scout around for things you might enjoy that could become part of your new lifestyle. New activities, restaurants, and nearby places to travel can take a bite out of your budget; don't feel like you have to see everything in the first month.

MY EXPERIENCE

Our first year in Seattle was the most exciting of our lives. It felt like an extended vacation. We had made a long list of tourist activities, and every weekend we made sure to do something on that list. Even when we weren't doing something from a tourist guidebook, we were out and about, walking in a neighborhood we hadn't visited, sitting on park benches we'd never sat in, hiking up mountains we'd never climbed before.

Just walk, bike, bus, or drive around your neighborhood to see what you can find. Some people give themselves plenty of time to get lost on purpose and explore.

Discover a new favorite restaurant. Don't just go to Applebee's because you had one in your old hometown—try the local place you've never been to. Check out nearby restaurants, and use online rankings to find some well-liked places in any price range of any type of food. The local newspaper or weekly alternative paper will list restaurants too, as well as live music, galleries, and literary events.

Feel free to ask people you meet for recommendations. While their interests may be different than yours, it's a great way to connect with people.

Meeting People

An important part of a healthy and fulfilling life is having close friends and family. It can be a daunting and lonely endeavor to start making a whole new set of connections. If you don't get to know people easily, this can be intimidating and the hardest part of getting settled. If you're part of a small minority in your new area, this can be even more difficult.

Depending on the surrounding culture and the neighborhood, and whether you're in an apartment or single-family home, you may not even see your neighbors during the first month—or you could find a welcome basket on your porch and people dropping by to meet you.

To become comfortable as a new resident, make an effort to stay active and try to meet people. If you're introverted, push yourself to talk to people more than you normally do.

Reach out to anyone you already have a connection with, however distant. There might be an old family friend, a cousin you've never met, a neighbor you knew when you were growing up, or your best friend's uncle. Meet for coffee; call them with questions. Most people are glad to be able to provide friendship and resources, whether or not you become lasting friends.

> MY EXPERIENCE
>
> *Prior to our move, we had not heard of the "Seattle Freeze," but we learned about it once we arrived. It's a local culture phenomenon that describes how it can be difficult for newcomers to make friends. While it feels like most of the people we've met have also been transplants, making deep and lasting friendships wasn't as easy as I'd hoped.*
>
> *If I were to do it again, I would try harder to put ourselves out there and find situations where we could get to know other people. I will say things have gotten much easier since we've had our first child, as babies and pets are people magnets.*

Where to Meet People

Here are some suggested places and methods to get to know more local people:

- **Contact acquaintances:** Reach out to acquaintances you may have met before; see if they are willing to get together for coffee.

- **Meet people at work:** If you have a job, your work place may be the easiest place to meet people. Although some prefer not to socialize too closely with their coworkers, at the very least, they could point you to some local opportunities to socialize.

- **Housewarming party:** You could invite neighbors, coworkers, anyone else you know in the area, and any out-of-town visitors you have. This could be hard to pull together, but if you promise (and provide) plenty of food and drinks, people will have an incentive to come. If you're afraid that people will be deterred because they'll think you expect gifts, ask them not to bring anything. Schedule it on a weekend and not too late. If you schedule it for a few weeks after you move in, it will motivate you to get everything put away and have your home organized!

- **Events:** In a local newspaper or on a blog, read the entertainment listings for nightlife or other social activities to find places to meet others. Maybe there's a bar that hosts a trivia night, or there might be groups that meet at the library or bookstore. Find the bulletin boards around town to see what's available.

- **Local organizations:** Look for local organizations to join, such as the nearest alumni chapter for your alma mater. Your Chamber of Commerce can be a good resource for this type of information. Professional networking events or conferences can help you make contacts. A local religious organization could offer a stimulating community. Some civic groups hold periodic "newcomers coffees."

- **Spend time in places:** Try to find a favorite "third place" (a place that isn't home or work), like a coffee shop, bar, bagel shop, or bookstore where you can hang out regularly.

- **Hobbies and interests:** Hobbies and interests can help you get to meet people. Meetup or other online groups can be a way to connect with complete strangers who are seeking connections around a shared interest, such as a wine tasting group or a knitting group. Check the local community center for classes and activities.

- **Online social media:** Who knows, you may strike up a Twitter conversation with someone who is attending the same event as you or meet someone who checked in at the same restaurant as you.

- **Activities for kids:** To help your children adjust, getting them enrolled in a summer camp or sports league will help them meet other kids while you make friends with other parents.

- **Chat up your neighbor:** Look for a good time to engage neighbors in conversation.

- **Look for excuses to talk to someone:** Take initiative to introduce yourself to others. If you've just moved in, knock on your neighbor's door and say hi. You could invite them over later to see your new place. Asking for directions is one way to start a conversation. Also, dogs and children are people magnets and great conversation starters.

Building Relationships with People

Some people can feel a sense of belonging by having a bunch of acquaintances; others prefer to establish fewer but deeper relationships. Here are some helpful tips for either preference:

- **Say it with body language:** Take an open body stance and make direct eye contact to show your interest in getting to know others.

- **Talk about being new:** When you meet someone, let them know that you've just moved there. They might ask questions and be eager to provide you with suggestions on some of the best the town has to offer, like grocery stores, medical care, and parks. If they're not forthcoming, you can try asking about things to do, places to eat, recommendations for a roofing company, and so on.

- **Look for things in common:** Build a connection with people by finding something you have in common and generating a conversation off that.

- **Accept invitations:** Now is the time to say yes to any invitations. You might rather be at home than go to a bar with your coworkers, but chances to socialize and build relationships with people can be infrequent and valuable, so it might be worth going. Remember: the more times you say no to an invitation, the less likely you will be invited in the future. Even if you don't click with the person who invites you, they might introduce you to others that you do get along with.

- **Child care:** If you have children, you're likely to meet other families through your kids. Take your children out to parks and playgrounds and see who you meet.

- **Persistence:** It can take a while to make friends, so look for recurring activities that will bring you in contact with the same people over time.

- **Regularity:** Go to the same places regularly—first, so that you feel comfortable in a familiar place, and second, so that people start to recognize you. By the fifth time you go to the coffee shop, the barista may recognize you. By the tenth time, other regulars may say hi and call you by name.

- **Don't take things too fast:** When you're new, it's tempting to trust anyone who is friendly to you. But take time to get to know them a little better. Take turns talking about yourself and being an interested listener.

- **Don't come on too strong**: People can be turned off if they sense that you're trying too hard and desperate for a new best friend. Look for cues that someone is done speaking and mentally come up with other things you could bring up next time you see them.

If making friends takes more effort than you expect, be patient. Be confident in your own "likeability" and don't worry.

Adjusting to a New Home

The first few weeks in a new place are like the honeymoon period of your relocation. After a while, some of the changes could become frustrating or uncomfortable and weigh you down; you might even dislike your new surroundings. Don't worry, this is a normal part of the adjustment process.

Give yourself time and try to avoid having more stress than you need. Although many things need to be done after moving in, you don't have to do everything at once. Maybe it's okay to leave those boxes in the corner until next weekend and go take a nap. Realize that in time, you will be able to accept the differences and begin to live with them.

Adapting to a Different Culture

If you have moved into a new regional culture, you'll probably pick up on some differences between the people here and the people you were used to "back home." This can be jarring if you are now immersed in a very different culture.

Regardless of how many miles you traveled to your new home, your "cultural distance" could be great and take some getting used to. Maybe you're not used to people who are so loud, talkative, judgmental, earnest, pushy, passive, self-interested, money-driven, unfriendly, pretentious, haughty, rude, or nice. Now, name whatever word is the opposite of what you think about them, and that might describe *the way they think about you!*

It may take a while to understand the people. For example, they don't mean to be rude, they're just direct in their communication. Or they're not unfriendly; they're just quiet until they get to know you.

Some of the differences can be minimal. Depending on where you are, people may use the words "soda," "pop," or "coke" for a carbonated soft drink.

Hopefully, you already observed some of these cultural differences in your research and previous visits, so you will be a little prepared. Make a concerted effort to be patient, open-minded, and flexible with the new people you meet.

Even after being in your new home for a while, you might occasionally feel like an outsider and miss aspects of your old home. However, the longer you spend in your new area, the more comfortable and familiar your surroundings will become.

Identity Changes

As you adjust to the new culture, you may notice changes in your identity. Your personal identity may be tied to your old hometown, a particular job, or things you used to do. Whatever reputation you had earned has disappeared, as people don't yet know you. This may feel like a loss, but it has a bright upside: this means that you are free to redefine yourself however you wish.

Over time, as the place becomes familiar, you should start to feel a sense of belonging.

MY EXPERIENCE

It took a while of living in Seattle before saying "We're from Texas" wasn't the first thing I said to people I met. Eventually I became comfortable telling people that I'm from Seattle when traveling out of town. Now when I say "I live in Seattle," that's part of my identity. A major milestone for me in becoming a Seattleite was when I was able to provide directions.

Track your journey of assimilation. Every three months, take a look at how far you've come using the Worksheet: Feelings About New Home.

It takes time to be at home in a new place, but eventually, you may come to identify more closely with your new home than with your old one. In fact, when going back to visit, you might experience *reverse* culture shock and notice things through different eyes. Find joy in the differences between people and places.

WORKSHEET: FEELINGS ABOUT NEW HOME

Use this worksheet to understand your feelings about your new home. Make copies of this worksheet and fill it out every three months.

What do you like most?

_____

What do you like least?

_____

What do you miss?

_____

What do you hope to do in the next three months?

_____

Children

Talk to your children regularly to learn how they are handling their new environment. Ask them anything about their new school: the classes, homework, teachers, kids, and what it's like. If you are able to listen without judgment and your child feels comfortable talking with you, you are more likely to be able to help them overcome any problems. If your child normally likes school and now doesn't want to go, find out what is bothering him.

If kids have difficult topics to discuss, don't gloss over them—find an appropriate way to open the discussion, understand what the issue is, and find out how you can help them fix it. Sometimes just your listening is all that is needed.

FAMILY AND FRIENDS

Staying in Contact

As you're settling in, you'll likely want to keep in touch with people "back home." This can provide significant social support. Today, with email, webcams, texting, and social networking, it's easy to stay connected and current.

As you go through the moving process, social media can keep your friends in the loop with your move. Or you may prefer sending a more traditional snail mail letter or post card from your new home. It could be fun to schedule an online video chat to update people and see some familiar faces.

> ## MY EXPERIENCE
>
> *We tried a few different approaches to keep in touch with family, like sending postcards, writing letters, making weekly phone calls, and scheduling regular Skype chats. Posting regularly on our blog also gave family and friends a place to go to know that we were doing well and enjoying ourselves. We've also taken contents from our blog, printed them out, and mailed them to my grandmother who doesn't use a computer. She loves the letters. All of these are not replacements for spending time in person with people, but they certainly help you keep in touch.*

You may feel pressure, or a desire, to let people visit you right away, but don't be afraid to ask for time to yourself. You may want to acclimate to your new home and learn your surroundings well enough to be able to show guests around town.

Visiting Home

If you've left family or friends behind at your previous home, you'll probably want to go back to visit from time to time.

Holidays can invite homesickness, especially if you will miss big traditional gatherings. It may be cost prohibitive to return for major holidays.

However, think about any special things you can do to create your own holiday celebrations. Perhaps you could host family to visit you on a holiday, or meet your family in a central location. You may spend a holiday with new friends.

Visiting old family and friends can be very stressful. People will probably be more excited to see you than ever before and your time will be limited.

MY EXPERIENCE

When Lesley and I visit, we have decided that a well-coordinated itinerary helps us make the most of our time and helps us to find time to spend with everyone. While we schedule plenty of leisurely family time, we also fit in time with friends. Then on long trips back, we set aside a day for us to be alone together. These visits also allow us to eat foods and go to places we enjoyed when we lived there.

When you do visit, you might stay with family or friends to make the most of the time back. It can be tempting to share all about your new place with everyone, especially if you love it. However, people's responses to your adventures might be all over the map. Be careful not to be too critical if you're now seeing things "back home" with fresher eyes.

On the other hand, if your adjustment to the new home has been rocky, you might feel overwhelmed with joy to be in your old home. It might seem better than you remembered, but remind yourself of the reasons why you decided to move in the first place.

COPING STRATEGIES

While the triumph of a successful move and the discovery of a new locale may deserve congratulations, losing your close connection to everything in your former place might be met with sympathy. In fact, moving can involve grief.

Within months of your arrival, the excitement diminishes and you settle into a daily routine. At that time, if you haven't been able to get comfortable and make good connections, you might start to feel a sense of loss for your old home.

There are suggestions to help you manage the transition to your new home. Of course, what works best for you will depend on your situation and personality:

- **Document your discoveries**: Take photos, share experiences on a blog, or post photos online as you explore your new area.

- **Be a cultural anthropologist**: Observe the differences from your old home. Adopting a detached and more scientific mindset may help you investigate and gain understanding. Study the culture and see what makes it different, even if you aren't able to embrace it.

- **Take the attitude of a problem solver:** List your challenges and then go through them one by one. What can you do? Think hard and be creative in developing solutions.

- **Write a journal of your feelings:** Just expressing your thoughts on paper or online may help you to understand and accept your feelings. How are you adjusting? What's changing?

- **Make goals:** What do you want to get done each day? Go to the public market? Take your new bike out? Go out with coworkers for lunch? Accomplishing your goals, however small they are, can help you to feel successful even if you're struggling in other areas of your life.

- **Make the most of where you are:** Enjoy what makes your location special and find ways to stretch yourself. Painting a picture, playing an instrument, or taking photos will focus your mind and add joy and beauty to your day. Taking up a new hobby or volunteering can help you feel reinvigorated. Joining a Pilates class, walking the dog, or lifting weights in the gym can improve your mood. Science proves that you can relieve stress just by spending time in nature: jogging on a trail, biking by the river, or sitting on a park bench.

- **Keep in touch with your past:** It may help to keep a foot in your old world as you reach out into the new one. Picking up the phone to chat with an old friend might put you in a better mood. It's wonderful to have someone you can vent to and laugh with. Sometimes all we need is a "witness," someone who really hears us.

- **Vent:** Write down all the things that you're not happy about in your new situation. If you can, tell someone. By getting things off your chest, you might find that things aren't as bad as you think.

- **Be patient:** It can take a long time to make friends, so be patient. It's tough to get by without the support network you used to have, so this can be a lonely time.

- **Look for humor:** Stay upbeat by finding things to laugh at, such as low-budget local commercials, anything outlandish, or amusing place names.

- **Accept what you can't change:** If there are things that bother you in your new home, you might just have to find a way to live with them.

- **Celebrate small victories:** Try to make the most out of each day. Look for little victories, such as finding a restaurant you like, saying hi to the neighbor, or going for a nice drive.

Support

Not having a group of people to support you can be difficult, especially if you face other challenges such as a death or illness in the family. Here are some tips for getting the support you need:

- **Medical resources:** If you have health challenges or are experiencing depression, your health care provider should be able to refer you to a support group. Even if you aren't an established patient, they can give you information about support groups. Additionally, groups like Alcoholics Anonymous and Weight Watchers can help if you are going through other challenges.

- **Local newspaper:** The events section of the newspaper (either printed or online) might include support group meeting times and places.

- **United Way or other charities:** Find a list of local nonprofit agencies and see if any of them include support groups.

- **Religious organizations:** There might be small groups available that meet in someone's home where people can be open with each other. It can be gratifying to share what's going on in a safe environment.

- **Meetup groups:** Your city might have groups of recent transplants that gather occasionally. Finding others who are going through similar challenges can help.

If homesickness persists and results in bad habits that affect your ability to function normally, please seek professional help. Check with your doctor or look for insurance coverage.

Even if your new home presents challenges, if you're patient you can learn to accept it as your home.

At some point, it may stop being "the place where you live now" and just turn into "home." If you're there long enough, maybe it'll even become "home sweet home."

LOOKING FORWARD

Personal influences

Moving not only changes your surroundings but it changes you as well. Everything affects your way of thinking and seeing the world: the environment you're exposed to, the people you meet, what you experience.

The more time you spend in your new hometown, the more that environment will influence you. Eventually, you will perceive everything around you as a new "normal."

To help track the changes in your world and how you are changing, fill out Worksheet: Changes After Moving.

WORKSHEET: CHANGES AFTER MOVING

This worksheet can help you identify ways that you've changed, explore what has influenced you, and understand your feelings.

HOW HAVE YOU AND YOUR LIFE CHANGED?	WHAT HAS CAUSED THIS CHANGE?	HOW DO YOU FEEL ABOUT THIS CHANGE?

My Experience

It amazes me sometimes how much of an impact that original thought to move away from home has had on me. More than six years after moving to Seattle, there's no question that moving has been a source of positive growth and experience in our lives.

For a few years, the process of moving to Seattle was the defining event of our lives, and we still felt like we had just moved here. Eventually, we realized that we are just living our lives here.

What next?

After finding and moving to the city of your dreams, what will you do next?

This move could be simply a period of your life to assert your independence and find yourself. It could be the first step in creating a new you. Will you settle down here, head back to familiar lands after a spell, or move on to new adventures in new places?

After moving, hopefully you can change your life to be more of what you want—more fulfilling, more productive, more lucrative, and more satisfying. With the right environment, relationships, scenery, living situation, and good fortune, your life will change in ways you want it to.

Perhaps the adventure of the move and excitement of living in a new place is enough motivation to repeat the process. Anywhere will become familiar after a few years; moving again can be a way to continue to learn about yourself and discover the world.

You're in charge

Regardless of what happens next, just relocating is a big accomplishment.

While where you live is important and changing your location can enhance your life, I hope your experience of moving shows that *you're in control of your life.*

By relocating, you grab the steering wheel from the forces of momentum and apathy and chart your own course. Whether you have a map of where you're going doesn't matter.

What matters is that *you* are behind the wheel. Every decision you make affects your trajectory and can teach you something and help you grow.

Your life is what you make of it, wherever you choose to live.

Online Resources

Visit www.ARelocationHandbook.com to download the worksheets in this book and access an up-to-date array of resources.

Some online resources are included for your reference. A link is not necessarily a recommendation.

EVALUATE AREAS AND HOMES

Learn About Different Places

- **Sperling's Best Places**
  www.bestplaces.net
  Data on towns and cities throughout the country, as well as a comparison feature, and comments from local residents.

- **City-Data.com**
  www.city-data.com
  Information on cities and towns across the nation, an active online forum, and some tools to help you plan your move.

- **ZIPskinny**
  www.zipskinny.com
  Location data website organized by zip codes with graphs that help in comparing locations to average or to other locations.

- **StreetAdvisor**
  www.streetadvisor.com
  Ratings, reviews, and photographs of city neighborhoods.

- **MetroTrends**
  datatools.metrotrends.org/charts/metrodata/Dashboard/v2/
  Graphs with key information including unemployment and jobs,
  housing costs, demographics, and crime.

Data Sources and Home Search

- **Walk Score**
  www.walkscore.com
  This website started by providing a "Walk Score" to quantify the
  convenience of walking to day-to-day destinations from any address.
  Now it provides rankings of the most walkable cities, towns, and
  neighborhoods and a walkability heat map. There is also an apartment
  search tool you can use to find homes in your price range that are in a
  conveniently walkable location.

- **Zillow**
  www.zillow.com
  Real estate website that includes search tools for real estate listings
  and includes their own home value estimate called "Zestimate." The
  website also includes a real estate agent database, mortgage
  calculators, forums, city data, and home design tips.

- **Trulia**
  www.trulia.com
  Real estate website that displays crime information, schools,
  amenities, real estate costs, demographic information, natural
  disaster risk, and other information on maps to help you find the best
  area for you.

- **Redfin**
  www.redfin.com
  Home search tool and real estate broker. The App can be useful to get
  a sense of real estate prices when traveling.

- **PadMapper**
  www.padmapper.com
  Apartment search engine that aggregates rental listings from other
  sites and maps them.

- **HotPads**
  www.hotpads.com
  Search aggregator of homes for sale as well as rentals.

- **Estately**
  www.estately.com
  Search for homes for sale using standard criteria as well as Walk Score.

- **realtor.com**
  www.realtor.com
  Real estate and apartment search site.

- **ApartmentRatings**
  www.apartmentratings.com
  Reviews of many larger apartment communities.

- **Vacation Rentals by Owner**
  www.vrbo.com
  Online listings to find a place to stay for visiting your new town.

- **Airbnb**
  www.airbnb.com
  Popular website to rent somewhere to stay from a local host.

CRITERIA

Employment

- **United States Department of Labor: Unemployment Rates for Metropolitan Areas**
  www.bls.gov/web/metro/laummtrk.htm
  Ranking of metropolitan areas by current unemployment rate.

- **Glassdoor Job Explorer**
  www.glassdoor.com/jobs/explorer/
  Map-based explorer that shows which parts of the country have the most open positions for the job title you enter.

Cost of Living Calculators

- **Bankrate Cost of Living Calculator**
  www.bankrate.com/calculators/savings/moving-cost-of-living-calculator.aspx
  Compares various costs of living between two cities.

- **Numbeo**
  www.numbeo.com
  Detailed cost of living data as well as information on property prices, crime, health care, pollution, traffic, travel costs, and quality of life.

Tax Information

- **Tax-Rates.org**
  www.tax-rates.org
  Information on sales tax, property tax, income tax, and business tax by state.

Crime

- **SpotCrime Crime Map**
  www.spotcrime.com
  Displays crimes that have been committed recently near any address you enter.

Natural Disaster Risk

- **NYTimes.com: Where to Live to Avoid a Natural Disaster**
  www.nytimes.com/interactive/2011/05/01/weekinreview/01safe.html
  Map of the US showing high-risk areas for tornados, hurricanes, and earthquakes.

Health

- **State of the Air**
  www.stateoftheair.org
  American Lung Association website with information on air quality by city. Cities are ranked by air quality, and there is also a tool to compare air quality in different locations as well as more information on air pollutants.

- **AIRNow**
  www.airnow.gov
  Current Air Quality Index by location and displayed on a U.S. map.

- **US Health Map | Institute for Health Metrics and Evaluation**
  vizhub.healthdata.org/us-health-map/
  Data visualization that shows key health indicators like life expectancy and rates of various diseases overlaid on a U.S. map.

- **Dartmouth Atlas of Health Care**
  www.dartmouthatlas.org/data/map.aspx?ind=143
  Variations in various health measures, such as number of physicians,
  mapped by locations.

Transportation

- **Google Maps**
  maps.google.com
  An indispensable resource for its maps, database of establishments,
  and Street View that allows you to see things at street level pretty
  much anywhere in the country.

- **Wikipedia: Transportation in the United States**
  en.wikipedia.org/wiki/Transportation_in_the_United_States
  Provides a lot of information, including commute patterns by city.

- **Wikipedia: Modal share**
  en.wikipedia.org/wiki/Modal_share
  Data on how people commute to work (whether by driving, walking,
  cycling, or taking public transportation) in select cities.

Education

- **Nation's Report Card**
  www.nationsreportcard.gov
  Scores students in various subjects and provides score variations
  across states, in major cities, and over a period of time.

- **Great Schools**
  www.greatschools.org
  School listing resource with reviews from parents and rankings of
  many schools.

Climate

- **CityRating.com Weather History**
  www.cityrating.com/weather-history/
  Graphs average weather by month, including temperatures, humidity,
  cloud conditions, rainfall, and number of days with extreme
  temperatures.

- **Allergy Capitals**
  www.allergycapitals.com
  Ranking of allergens by city.

- **Pollen.com**
  www.pollen.com
  Daily information about allergies and pollen counts.

Recreation

- **Volunteering in America**
  www.volunteeringinamerica.gov
  Information on volunteering, including rankings of volunteerism by state.

- **Interactive: How America Gives – The Chronicle of Philanthropy**
  www.philanthropy.com/article/Interactive-How-America-Gives/133709
  Map of donation rates by state.

Demographics

- **Same-Sex Couple Households**
  www.census.gov/prod/2011pubs/acsbr10-03.pdf
  Percentage of same-sex couple households by state.

Decision-Making

- **Wikipedia: Analytic Hierarchy Process**
  en.wikipedia.org/wiki/Analytic_Hierarchy_Process
  This process lets you apply your criteria and sub-criteria to the options you're considering. It's a more complex way to decide but is a more structured framework that results in a decision.

MOVING ABROAD

- **About.com Move Overseas**
  moving.about.com/od/internationalmoves/
  A variety of resources and information on moving internationally.

- **Expat Exchange**
  www.expatexchange.com
  Resources for prospective or current expatriates to learn about other cultures, address numerous details required for an international move, and learn from others' experiences.

- **Pilot Guides**
  www.pilotguides.com

Geared towards travelers; has videos, articles, and news about destinations all over the world.

- **CountryReports**
  www.countryreports.org
  Information on cultures and countries around the world available for a fee.

- **Country Watch**
  www.countrywatch.com
  Detailed information on countries available for a fee.

- **Property Abroad**
  www.property-abroad.com
  View homes for sale internationally.

- **EscapeArtist**
  www.escapeartist.com
  Aims to be a resource for those moving internationally and features properties for sale all over the world.

- **U.S. State Department Country Information**
  travel.state.gov/content/passports/english/country.html
  Information for every country in the world, including the location of the U.S. embassy and information about whether you need a visa, as well as health and safety information.

- **Office of Overseas Schools**
  www.state.gov/m/a/os/
  International schools that meet educational standards of the U.S. State Department.

- **RIM / International ProMover**
  www.promover.org/rim_intl
  The Registered International Mover program has established standards for professionalism and ethics.

PLANNING

For Budgeting Home Fees and Closing Costs

- **How to buy a house**
  www.michaelbluejay.com/house/
  A guide for first-time homebuyers that includes a closing cost

calculator as well as a lot of other information to help you plan for your home purchase.

- **Zillow: Buyers' Closing Costs Breakdown**
  www.zillow.com/wikipages/Buyers%27-Closing-Costs-Breakdown/
  Outline of typical closing costs that a buyer should expect to pay.

Finding an Occupation

- **About.com Job Searching**
  jobsearch.about.com
  Information, tools, and resources for finding a job.

- **Quintessential Careers**
  www.quintcareers.com
  Job search resource with articles and tools.

- **Salary.com**
  www.salary.com
  Features salary information for the U.S. and Canada as well as job postings and tools to help you with your career.

- **Indeed**
  www.indeed.com
  Job search engine that aggregates job listings from thousands of websites and is currently the most popular job website.

- **Glassdoor**
  www.glassdoor.com
  Job search engine with reviews of employers.

- **Monster.com**
  www.monster.com
  Job board with other career resources, including message boards and advice from experts.

- **Careerbuilder.com**
  www.careerbuilder.com
  Job board with resources, including information about applicants applying for the same job as you.

- **SimplyHired**
  www.simplyhired.com
  Job search engine that aggregates job listings.

ARRANGING YOUR MOVE

Resources

- **My Move**
  www.mymove.com
  Tools, calculators, and how-to resources for relocating.

- **About.com Moving**
  moving.about.com
  Tools, resources, and links to help you move.

Finding Movers

- **Movers**
  www.movers.com
  Provides quotes for moving your things and your car both
  domestically and internationally as well as numerous moving guides.

- **Moving.com**
  www.moving.com
  Connects to rental truck companies, self-storage warehouses, movers,
  and car-transport companies. Includes tools and online calculators to
  help you plan and price your move as well as data and resources on
  towns and cities across the country.

- **American Moving and Storage Association**
  www.moving.org
  Includes estimating tool and links to professional movers and
  information to prepare for your move as well as an Ask the Expert
  service.

- **MovingMatrix.com**
  www.movingmatrix.com
  Website for soliciting quotes for moves.

- **National Association of Senior Move Managers**
  www.nasmm.org
  Association that helps senior adults relocate.

- **100 Largest Moving Companies of the U.S. and Canada**
  www.movingcompanyreviews.com/articles/100-largest-moving-
  companies-of-the-us-and-canada/
  Tool for identifying the biggest moving companies.

Choosing Movers

- **Better Business Bureau**
  www.bbb.org
  Resource for researching apartment-management companies and movers.

- **Your Rights and Responsibilities When You Move**
  www.protectyourmove.gov/documents/Rights-and-Responsibilities-2013.pdf
  Information on selecting a mover, coverage for damage, paperwork, and other topics to be aware of when moving.

Mover Complaints

- **National Customer Complaint Database**
  nccdb.fmcsa.dot.gov
  U.S. Department of Transportation website for reporting "safety, service or discrimination issues with a moving company, bus or truck company."

- **Bureau of Consumer Protection**
  www.ftc.gov/about-ftc/bureaus-offices/bureau-consumer-protection
  Another path for submitting complaints against a mover.

- **DOT Company Search**
  ai.volpe.dot.gov/hhg/search.asp
  Information including complaint and safety history for any interstate movers.

- **National Association of Attorneys General**
  www.naag.org
  Use this website to find the Attorney General in your state and contact them to file complaints against an unlawful mover.

Moving a Pet

- **GoPetFriendly.com**
  www.gopetfriendly.com
  The website includes a road trip planning tool that helps you find user-submitted references on pet-friendly restaurants, hotels, and other establishments and services across the country.

- **PetTravel.com**
  www.pettravel.com
  A resource for traveling with your pets, including airline rules and information for bringing your pet into any other country.

- **Dog Jaunt Airport Pet Relief Areas**
  www.dogjaunt.com/guides/airport-pet-relief-areas/
  Guidance on traveling with your pet that focuses on dogs and includes locations of airport pet relief areas.

- **Happy Tails Travel**
  www.happytailstravel.com
  Offers pet relocation services.

MOVING OUT

Planning a Road Trip

- **Fuel Cost Calculator**
  www.fuelcostcalculator.com
  Tool to estimate fuel costs for your relocation road trip.

Preparing to Pack

- **UsedCardboardBoxes.com**
  www.usedcardboardboxes.com
  Buy boxes and packing kits for your move.

For Selling Your Home and Disposing of Your Things

- **Homethinking**
  www.homethinking.com
  Resources to find realtors in your area based on ratings and past sales.

- **Earth911.com**
  www.earth911.com
  Environmental reference site includes information on where to recycle household goods.

ARRIVING AND SETTLING IN

Voting and Taxes

- **Register to Vote**
  www.eac.gov/voter_resources/register_to_vote.aspx
  Voter registration for your new location.

- **IRS Publication 521, Moving Expenses**
  www.irs.gov/uac/Publication-521,-Moving-Expenses
  Information about deducting your moving costs when submitting
  your taxes.

- **IRS Publication 529, Miscellaneous Deductions**
  www.irs.gov/uac/Publication-529,-Miscellaneous-Deductions
  Information about deducting your job search expenses.

Explore Your New Area

- **Meetup**
  www.meetup.com
  Site for finding activities with other people in your area who share
  your interests.

- **TripAdvisor**
  www.tripadvisor.com
  Resource to discover attractions in your new hometown as a tourist.

- **Yelp**
  www.yelp.com
  Includes reviews of local establishments. Reviews of movers and
  apartment buildings might also be helpful in planning your move.

- **Citysearch**
  www.citysearch.com
  Tool to find restaurants, nightlife, shopping, and services to try in your
  new home.

Commercial Offers

- **National Do Not Call Registry**
  www.donotcall.gov
  Government website for registering your new phone number to avoid
  telemarketing calls.

- **DMAchoice**
  www.dmachoice.org
  Similar to the National Do Not Call Registry, but for opting out of types of mail that you're not interested in receiving.

Reference Books

The following list includes books that you might find helpful for your move. Many of these influenced this book or were cited in this book.

- *Who's Your City?: How the Creative Economy Is Making Where to Live the Most Important Decision of Your Life*
Richard Florida

- *Newcomer's Handbooks:* www.newcomershandbooks.com

- *Making the Big Move: How to Transform Relocation into a Creative Life Transition*
Cathy Goodwin

- *The Big Sort: Why the Clustering of Like-Minded America is Tearing Us Apart*
Bill Bishop

- *After the Boxes Are Unpacked: Moving On After Moving In*
Susan Miller

- *But Mom, I Don't Want to Move!*
Susan Miller

- *How to Survive a Move: by Hundreds of Happy People Who Did and Some Things to Avoid, From a Few People Who Haven't Unpacked Yet*
Jaime Miller

- *Strategic Relocation—North American Guide to Safe Places*
  Joel M. Skousen

- *Making Your Move to One of America's Best Small Towns: How to Find a Great Little Place as Your Next Home Base*
  Norman Crampton

- *Six Thinking Hats*
  Edward de Bono

- *Success Principles*
  Jack Canfield

- *Stumbling on Happiness*
  Daniel Gilbert

Works Cited

Brinkhoff, Thomas. 2014. *Major Agglomerations of the World.* July 1. Accessed November 3, 2014. http://www.citypopulation.de/world/Agglomerations.html.

Council on Graduate Medical Education. 1996. "Patient Care Physician Supply and Requirements: Testing COGME Recommendations." Accessed 11 2, 2014. http://www.hrsa.gov/advisorycommittees/bhpradvisory/cogme/Repor ts/eighthreport.html.

Crispin, Gerry and Mark Mehler. 2014. "Source of Hire Report." *CareerXroads.* September. Accessed November 3, 2014. http://www.careerxroads.com/news/2014_SourceOfHire.pdf.

Florida, Richard. 2008. *Who's Your City?* Basic Books.

Friedman, Richard A., M.D. 2007. "Brought on by Darkness, Disorder Needs Light." *New York Times*, December 18. http://www.nytimes.com/2007/12/18/health/18mind.html.

Nahajewski, Allan. 2012. "Homing in on a Recovering Market." *Deliver Magazine*, May: 9.

Powdthavee, Nattavudh. 2007. *Putting a Price Tag on Friends, Relatives, and Neighbours: Using Surveys of Life Satisfaction to Value Social Relationships.* London: Journal of Socio-Economics.

Siniavskaia, Natalia, Ph.D. 2008. "Spending Patterns of Home Buyers." http://www.nahb.org/generic.aspx?sectionID=734&genericContentID=106491&channelID=311.

U.S. Census. 2011. "City & Towns Totals: Vintage 2011 - U.S Census Bureau." *U.S. Census Bureau.* July 1. Accessed November 3, 2014. http://www.census.gov/popest/data/cities/totals/2011/files/SUB-EST2011-IP.csv.

—. 2013. "Table 23. Reason for Move, by Sex, Age, Race and Hispanic Origin, Relationship to Householder, Educational Attainment, Marital Status, Nativity, Tenure, Poverty Status, and Type of Move (All Categories): 2012 to 2013." *U.S. Census Bureau.* November. Accessed November 2, 2014. https://www.census.gov/hhes/migration/files/cps/cps2013/tab23-3.xls.

—. 2013. "Table 24. Reason for Move of Movers 16 Years and Over, by Household Income in 2012, Labor Force Status, Major Occupation Group, Major Industry Group, and Type of Move (All Categories): 2012 to 2013." *U.S. Census Bureau.* November. Accessed November 2, 2014. https://www.census.gov/hhes/migration/files/cps/cps2013/tab24-3.xls.

—. 2011. "Table 38. Native and Foreign-Born Population by Place of Birth and State: 2009." *U.S. Census Bureau.* September 30. Accessed November 1, 2014. http://www.census.gov/compendia/statab/2012/tables/12s0038.xls.

Made in the USA
Coppell, TX
20 October 2021

64386581R00144